THE
WRITER'S
VOICE

Also by Anne Janzer

Other books in The Writer's Process series

The Writer's Process: Getting Your Brain in Gear

The Writer's Process Workbook: Simple Practices for Finding Your Best Process

The Workplace Writer's Process: A Guide to Getting the Job Done

Other books

Writing to Be Understood: What Works and Why

Get the Word Out: Write a Book That Makes a Difference

33 Ways Not to Screw Up Your Business Emails

Subscription Marketing: Strategies for Nurturing Customers in a World of Churn

THE WRITER'S VOICE

TECHNIQUES FOR TUNING YOUR TONE AND STYLE

ANNE JANZER

Cuesta Park Consulting

Scotts Valley, California
Copyright © 2023 by Anne Janzer

Printed in the United States of America

Print ISBN 978-1-952284-10-6
Ebook ISBN: 978-1-952284-11-3

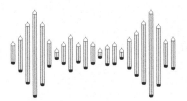

Contents

Introduction: Voice Is a Choice 1

    What Do We Mean by "Writing Voice?" 3

    A Practical Definition 4

    The Muse, the Scribe, and Your Voice 5

    How to Use This Book 6

    Ground Rules 7

Initial Self-Assessment 9

Week 1: Listen to the Inner Reader 11

    Read Your Words Aloud 13

    Narrate Another Writer's Work 14

    Explore What *Not* to Do 16

    Listen to Automated Narration 17

    This Week 19

Week 2: Pick Words That Pack a Punch 21

    Whittle Down the Weak Words 23

    Swap In Shorter Words 24

    Look Around for Similar Sounds 29

    Words That Create Character 32

    This Week 34

Week 3: Track the Punctuation Prints 35

    Writing Without Words 36

    Compare Your Punctuation Across Formats 37

    Peruse Other Writers' Punctuation 38

    This Week 39

Week 4: Find Your Sentence Rhythm 41

    The Basic Sentence Exercise 43

    Scope Other Authors' Sentences 45

    Alternating Sentence Lengths 46

    Your Ideal Sentence Ratio 48

    This Week 49

Week 5: Compose Paragraph Patterns 51
   Peruse Paragraph Patterns 53
   Rearrange for Effect 55
   Write to a Paragraph Pattern 58
   This Week 59

Week 6: Readability 61
   Check Your Readability Level 63
   Make It More Readable 64
   Make Your Work *Less* Readable 65
   Check Other Writers' Readability 66
   This Week 67

Week 7: State Your Intentions 69
   Who Do You Serve and How? 72
   Inform, Persuade, Entertain 75
   Letter to the Author 78
   This Week 80

Week 8: You as a Fictional Character 81
   Sketch Your Character 83
   Pick Three Adjectives 86
   Try On Another Character 88
   This Week 90

Week 9: Presence or Absence 91
   Disappear Entirely 93
   Be Too Intrusive 95
   Violate Expectations 96
   This Week 97

Week 10: Relating to the Reader 99
   Formal, Informal, Intimate, or Distant 99
   Getting Personal with Pronouns 101
   Fancy or Folksy 103
   Expert to Companion 107
   This Week 110

Week 11: Your Tone, Their Mood 111
   Expressing a Clear Tone 113
   Be a Moody Reader 116
   This Week 117

Week 12: Moving Closer with Emotion 119
   Spreading Emotions Through Story 120
   Emotional Drafting 121
   Emotions in the Text 123
   Sticky Stories 124
   This Week 126

CONTENTS

Putting These Techniques to Work 127

    Tuning Your Own Voice 127

    Ghostwriting 128

    Brand Voice 129

    Fictional Characters 130

    The Occasional Refresher or Spark of Inspiration 130

What About AI? 131

Closing Assessment 133

Acknowledgments 135

Further Reading 137

About the Author 139

Voice Is a Choice

New writers often struggle to achieve a unique and *authentic* voice in their work. If you've been writing for a while, you have probably developed a distinct, comfortable writing voice. These habits become ingrained over time.

The concept of writing voice is nebulous. Does your writing voice live in the words on the page? Is it an inherent part of your personality as a writer or merely a bag of stylistic tricks? What role does the reader play in determining voice?

To better understand these questions, I surveyed more than 250 writers, asking questions about how they felt about their voice, how they controlled it, and what they would change if they could. The results shed light on this little-appreciated, often-overlooked part of the writing craft.

On a scale of 1 to 5, how happy are you with your writing voice and how it represents you and your ideas?

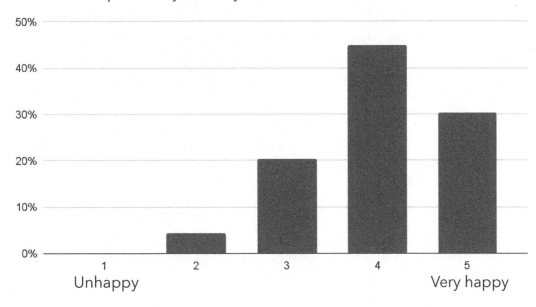

Most people reported feeling satisfied with their writing voices.[1]

You might think I would have abandoned this book entirely at that point. But wait, there's more!

Few of the respondents actively controlled or modified their voice, beyond making minor edits in revision. Fewer than one in five could easily shift the way their writing sounded. A few people commented that they never really thought about their writing voice before taking the survey.

Despite the reported satisfaction, most people also wished for writing that was:

- More compelling or riveting

- More fluid and relaxed

- Funnier or lighter

- More interesting/less boring

- Smoother/less awkward

How about you? Are you searching for an authentic voice? Are you generally satisfied with the way you write, while harboring a bothersome sense that you could improve?

If you keep writing the same way you always have, you're like an athlete who only runs, without stretching or cross-training. When you go to that first yoga class or try rock climbing, you're going to suffer. If you want to take full advantage of your body's capabilities, you should stretch and strengthen in multiple directions.

The same is true for writers. Even if we rely on a consistent professional or personal writing voice, by stretching and exploring we discover fresh possibilities in our writing.

This workbook is a comprehensive writing voice workout. Use the tools and techniques here to hunt for an authentic voice, or to uncover aspects of your authentic voice that you have not explored. You may even become part of that elite minority of writers who master the ability to shift their voice easily. When this happens, your writing life opens up in interesting ways. Heck, it becomes more fun.

That's been my experience, at any rate.

Before I started writing books, I was a *writing chameleon* (a term I just made up). I shifted my writing voice to match the needs of my rotating roster of technology

---

1 This data comes from a survey I conducted in early 2023. More than 250 writers responded. You can find the survey results on my website at AnneJanzer.com/writing-voice-survey-results.

clients—ghostwriting for an executive one day, creating a brand voice on a website the next. I loved the challenge.

This experience fed my fascination with what *voice* really means in writing and set me exploring the science and art of writing voice. As I compiled the research, I realized it wasn't enough. Instead of reading, we need to experiment with voice. I crafted and tested exercises to explore the various levers that act on our writing voices. You hold the result in your hands.

Having a wide variety of voices at your command is like having a refrigerator full of fresh ingredients ready to cook with. You'll create better work.

What Do We Mean by "Writing Voice?"

Let's start with the metaphor itself. Because written language evolved from speaking, we borrow the metaphor of the speaking voice to describe how we "sound" in our writing. This metaphor works on many levels.

Our voices are unique to us.

When a friend or family member says "Hello" on the phone, you can probably identify them without seeing the name on the display. Even with the limited audio quality, we connect the sound with the person. Banks often use voice as a biometric identification factor—like a fingerprint—to confirm identity.

Similarly, we can often recognize the writing of favorite authors. Many literary writers and poets take pride in their unique voices. The field of forensic linguistics specializes in identifying people from their written work.

We adjust our voices naturally.

We learn to vary our speaking voices based on the situation, starting from a young age. ("*Use your indoor voice!*") We speak tenderly to an ailing child and loudly in front of a roomful of people.

Our written voices are similarly flexible. We use a different tone for a text message to a friend from what we use for a letter to the CEO. This comes naturally.

We can extend our natural capabilities.

With work, we can train our physical voices to do remarkable things, like holding people spellbound with Hamlet's soliloquy, singing coloratura arias, or beatboxing.

Similarly, we can learn to write dialog for fictional characters or create a powerful "brand" voice for our employers. Some writers become adept at mimicking others—a talent that comes in handy for ghostwriting books or creating parodies.

We are not stuck with our default speaking or writing voices.

This book gives you tools to tune and transform your writing voice. Perhaps you will become more confident in the way your writing represents you in the world. You may become so adept that you can choose a voice to fit the situation as easily as you choose a jacket for the weather.

A Practical Definition

Let's define what we're talking about. Writing voice does not depend on a speaking voice—the metaphor does not extend that far. A brand may have a fun, distinctive voice, but we don't expect everyone who works for that company to speak that way. A chatbot has no physical speaking apparatus, yet may seem to have a "voice" in the written word.

Nonhuman voices or fictional characters don't have physical voices. But they do have a voice in the writing, as long as we perceive one when reading.

That's the secret. We can argue over whether voice lives in our authentic selves or the stylistic flourishes on the page. Ultimately, the writer's voice takes shape in the reader's head.

Let's work with the following simple definition:

> Writing voice is the persona that the reader detects when reading words.

This broad definition fits many genres and situations:

- Poetic voice

- Fictional characters

- Brand voice

- Professional writing

Using this definition, the *reader* determines your writing voice. You cannot implant it in people's heads unless you record a narration. As the writer, author, and teacher Ben Yagoda writes, "Even the most thoughtful writers can stare at a sentence for a whole day and not realize precisely how readers will 'hear' it."[2]

Most of us have much more control over our readers' perception than we choose to exert. The late writing teacher Don Fry[3] defined writing voice this way:

> Voice is the sum of writing strategies that creates the illusion that the writer is speaking directly to the reader from the page or screen.

---

2 This quote comes from Yagoda's excellent book *The Sound on the Page*, a deep dive into literary voice.

3 Roy Peter Clark of the Poynter Institute shared this definition with me: he has used it since learning it from Don.

By this definition, voice originates in writing strategies. And this book suggests a number of these strategies and techniques. To take control of our voices, we need to exercise both our analytical and creative, intuitive powers.

The Muse, the Scribe, and Your Voice

Before you set out to discover the range and possibilities of your writing voice, consider your companions on this task: your Muse and your Scribe.

These two inner characters appeared in *The Writer's Process*. If you haven't read that book, let me introduce you. The Muse and Scribe are useful fictions that embody distinct sets of cognitive processes involved in writing. By imagining them as separate aspects of ourselves, we can identify the processes and attitudes we need to bring to the work.

The Muse represents your inner creative self. It contributes ideas, words, and images. New projects thrill the Muse. It often thinks in associations or wild leaps, rarely following a linear path. The Muse infuses our work with energy and meaning. Because it falls outside our intentional control, it seems mysterious, fickle, and perhaps godlike. In Greek mythology, the Muses were gods protecting the arts.

The Scribe's job is less glamorous but equally important, because the Scribe gets the writing done. It schedules the work, wrestles ideas into an outline, and makes us sit with pen or keyboard at hand. It evaluates the result and takes the steps to complete projects.

The successful writer knows when to pass projects from one to the other and when they both need to collaborate. Most of us favor either the Muse or the Scribe and must learn how to support the less-active entity and keep the work in balance.[4] Most of the experiments in this book will appeal more to one or the other, but there will be plenty of opportunity for collaboration.

---

4 Do you have a shy Muse? Is your Muse temperamental or reliable? Take the short Muse Quiz at AnneJanzer.com/Muse-Quiz to explore your own.

How to Use This Book

As you complete this workbook, think of yourself as a mad scientist engaged in a series of experiments to deepen your understanding of your writing voice. Your two lab assistants are your Scribe (analytical and disciplined processes) and your Muse (creativity).

Here's what you'll need:

- Samples of your writing to work with.

- This workbook or a dedicated journal or online files to track your results and notice what's working.

You can approach this book as a twelve-week program, with one week dedicated to each specific approach to writing voice. Spending a full week gives you time to explore the techniques and notice how they show up in works by other writers you read.

But hey, no one's looking. You can also skip around and jump right to the approaches that interest you most. Race through the whole workbook in a few days, or spend the year dipping in. These tools don't expire, and you may find you want to revisit several of them.

If you choose to go through it in order, here's what you'll find.

Weeks 1 to 6 focus on the *outer* work of voice—what readers see on the page as words, sentences, and paragraphs. As you experiment with the ideas here, you'll see how relatively minor adjustments to basic stylistic decisions can have a major impact on how the reader detects the writer's voice. The Scribe is likely to take the lead on these tactics since they appeal to the analytical, critical mind.

Weeks 7 to 12 focus on the *inner* work of voice: your intentions and personality, your relationship with the reader, emotions, and more. Many of these tools work better when you apply them while drafting. Your Muse will take the lead.

You can repeat these experiments with multiple texts or writing prompts. At the end of each section, track which methods you found useful. Not all will resonate. A few may seem difficult or leave you cold. A few may become a permanent part of your writing toolkit, ready to help when you need guidance.

Ground Rules

No matter whether you work through all twelve weeks in order or skip around randomly, observe these three basic ground rules:

One: Bring an open mind.

You are conducting experiments in the craft of writing. Some will fail, others succeed. That's expected. You will hear negative self-talk. (*This is awful!*) You will write truly terrible sentences. Remind yourself that this is a metaphorical laboratory, and nothing will literally blow up. Go wild and focus on discovering rather than judging.

Two: Track what you learn.

Record your observations after each exercise. These notes will help when you revisit the workbook later. They will also keep you grounded in a mindset of experimentation and growth.

Three: Have fun.

For open writing prompts, don't be afraid to be ridiculous or go way too far. Release yourself from trying to get the voice "just right" as you experiment. Give the Muse free rein when drafting from scratch.

Several of the exercises ask you to work at absurd extremes. Intentionally going too far invites the creative Muse, and offers insight into the real range of possibilities.

Before you dive into the exercises, take the following self-assessment of where you are right now. Let's dive in.

Initial Self-Assessment

Before undertaking these experiments, take a few moments to think about how you feel about your writing voice. When you're done, you'll have a benchmark to see if you've made progress.

Satisfaction

Thinking about the writing you do most (or that is most important to you):

On a scale of 1 to 5, how happy are you with your writing voice and how it represents you and your ideas?

	1	2	3	4	5	
Not happy	○	○	○	○	○	Very happy

Overall, how much control do you think you have over your writing voice, on a scale of 1 to 5, with 1 being no control and 5 being complete control.

	1	2	3	4	5	
No control	○	○	○	○	○	Complete control

How would you finish the following sentence? Choose all that apply.

If I could change anything about my writing voice, I wish I could make it...

☐ More "like me"
☐ More casual
☐ More fluid and relaxed
☐ Easier to understand
☐ More authoritative or expert
☐ More educated
☐ Smoother/less awkward

☐ Funnier or lighter
☐ More beautiful/literary/poetic
☐ Less "corporate"
☐ More interesting/less boring
☐ More compelling or riveting
☐ I wouldn't change anything
☐ I already change the voice as needed

Is there anything I missed? Are there any other attributes you wish your writing voice embodied?

- _____
- _____
- _____

WEEK 1

Listen to the Inner Reader

Before printing presses and bookstores, people passed along stories as poems and songs so they might remember them. Today, with the growth in audiobooks, speech-to-text tools, and AI-based narration, we listen yet again to the written word.

Written language emerged from the rhythm and sound of speech. Yet we often forget about listening when we write, and neglect the sound of our words.

I ran headlong into this dilemma when narrating my first audiobook, *Subscription Marketing*. Because I had a "conversational" writing style, I figured it would be easy. Instead, I fell right into the chasm between speech and writing.

First, the word *subscription* trips up a tiring narrator. The consonants *b* and *p* test the pop filter on the mic. The hiss of the *s* sound makes the word messy. Try saying *subscription* five times quickly and you'll know what I mean.

Worse, the sentences didn't flow the way I'd hoped. They sounded better in my head. Narrating the audiobook made me reconsider my writing voice. Thinking of each book as a script has made me a better writer.

Even people who read silently likely listen to an inner narrator.

According to a study published in 2016, many people hear an inner voice as they read. That voice may not be their own. The psychologist who reported these findings refers to this as an *inner reading voice* and estimates that 70 percent of us hear one as we read.[5] Do you?

That inner narrator, like a real one, can trip over words. It might lose energy while slogging through dense prose. Try reading a phonetic description of a thick

---

5 For more on the inner reading voices, see the article "Inner Reading Voices" by Ruvanee P. Vilhauer in the journal *Psychosis*, 8:1, 37-41.

dialect and you'll realize how tiring it can be. Here's a snippet from Emily Brontë's *Wuthering Heights*, from a character (Joseph) who speaks in a Yorkshire dialect:

> "They's nobbutt t'misis, and shoo'll nut oppen't an ye mak yer flaysome dins til neeght."

Our brains have to sound out the words, then figure out what they mean and assemble them into sentences. It's hard cognitive work, and we're tempted to skip ahead.

Similarly, dense prose interrupts the reading flow. When the inner reading voice tires, the reader may lose the thread. To detect where that might happen, you'll need to *listen* to your work. The first technique in working with your writing voice is simply this: read and listen.

Read Your Words Aloud

Nearly every writing teacher suggests you read your work aloud.

That's the first, simplest technique in this book. Choose a few pages of your work and speak them. Don't rush through it, find a natural rhythm. Picture yourself narrating an audiobook or reading the work to a friend. If you're tempted to skip or hurry through sections, record yourself.

As you read, pay attention to the experience of narrating. What does it feel like? Where do you run into problems?

Notice how the piece sounds. Does the rhythm vary or does it sound monotonous? Do the important parts stand out?

Listen for clues about where to tinker with your writing so that it reads better.

NARRATING OBSERVATIONS

- Did you stumble or backtrack? If so, mark where that happened.

- Did you use inflection and emphasis to add meaning and navigate through the prose?

- Did you find strings of words hard to pronounce? If so, mark those areas.

- Did you run out of breath in a long sentence or have to break in an awkward place to breathe? If yes, mark where that happened in the text.

- Did you pause at the commas and between sentences?

- Did you take longer pauses between paragraphs?

LISTENING OBSERVATIONS

- How did it sound? How would you characterize the "feel" or tone of the piece?

- Did you detect a rhythm to the sentences or words?

- Did it hold your interest as you narrated?

- List anything you might want to change:

_____

_____

_____

Narrate Another Writer's Work

Now that you've experienced what it's like to read your own writing aloud, read other writers who work in your genre.

For example, if you want to write for a literary magazine, find other pieces in that journal. If you want to write children's fiction, pick a work by a favorite author. If you're writing a blog post, open one by a writer you admire.

Read it aloud as if you were narrating an audiobook. By doing this, you can get inside the narrator's voice and hear what's going on. You may notice things when reading aloud that you only register subconsciously when reading silently.

For example, you may suddenly discover that the work has a rhythm you hadn't noticed, or you might spot alliteration or internal rhyme in the prose.

Here are a few features to listen for:

- Does the writer play with the rhythm of the work by changing sentence lengths?

- Do you get stuck on certain words?

- Does it flow smoothly?

- How does the experience of reading this aloud differ from reading your own work?

You may admire authors you would never try to imitate or borrow from. That's fine. Even a brief study of excellent writing may reveal lessons about what works.

Try reading several authors and track your observations.

OBSERVATIONS

Author/work: _____

_____

What I noticed: _____

_____

What I'd like to try: _____

_____

Author/work: _____

_____

What I noticed: _____

_____

What I'd like to try: _____

_____

Explore What *Not* to Do

Just for fun, pick up something you do *not* enjoy reading: a legal contract, a chapter of a book you cannot get through, or a boring textbook.

Read a section aloud. Notice what trips you up. You may find clues here for why you don't like this piece, and what to avoid in your own writing.

OBSERVATIONS

Author/work: _____

_____

What I noticed: _____

_____

What I'd like to avoid: _____

_____

Author/work: _____

_____

What I noticed: _____

_____

What I'd like to avoid: _____

_____

Listen to Automated Narration

To hear the rhythm of the work without getting caught up in the meaning, let the computer read to you.

You have many options, including:

- Your phone or computer's text-to-speech capabilities (Look in the Accessibility options.)

- The Read Aloud feature in the Review area of Microsoft Word

- AI-based narration tools

You don't need to a text-to-speech program with lifelike results. A monotonous reader may help you better hear the rhythm inherent in the words.

First, gather several pieces of different types of writing. The contrast will help. Collect extracts from:

1. Your own writing

2. Other writers you admire in your genre

3. Business or professional writing

4. A paragraph from a legal contract. (Check the Terms and Conditions for your online apps.)

Use an automated narrator to listen to each, paying attention to the rhythm and sounds instead of the meaning. Does the work establish a cadence? Is it long and continuous, or do clauses give it bounce without disturbing the flow? Does it stutter and trip?

OBSERVATIONS

Sample: _____

_____

What I learned: _____

_____

Sample: _____

_____

What I learned: _____

_____

Sample: _____

_____

What I learned: _____

_____

▪▪▪ THIS WEEK:

READING: Every day, read aloud for a few minutes from different types of work: articles, blog posts, emails, books. Notice the rhythm and sound of the work.

WRITING: Experiment with reading your own work aloud as you write or revise. If you're writing emails, read them aloud before sending. Do you learn anything about the way your default writing voice sounds?

▪ ▪ ▪

WEEK 2

Pick Words That Pack a Punch

Poets analyze each word with care. You and I, writing prose, rarely have the time or inclination to do that. We choose our words for meaning, of course, and may neglect the way they sound on the page. We could learn from the poets by paying attention to the texture and sound of the words we use, and the rhythms they create.

Too often, we stuff our writing with the same old words we use everywhere else. This gets boring for readers and for us as well.

Swapping out a few words can alter the tone and rhythm of the work more than you might expect. Better yet, you can make these tuning adjustments during a quick revision. This strategy requires minimal effort and produces maximum results.

Which words should you replace? Here are a few candidates:

The usual, overused suspects: Most of us have a jar full of words that we pull from all the time when writing—like a chef who only seasons with salt.

For example, my first drafts swim in adjectives like *new*, *big*, and *some*. I also rely heavily on verbs like *start* and variations of *to be*. Replacing these passive verbs with active ones breathes life into sentences.

The repeaters: If the same noun or verb appears more than twice in a few sentences, consider replacing at least one occurrence.

Long words: Words with many syllables act like brakes for the inner reading voice, slowing the momentum through the sentence.

Words with 'tion' endings: These nouns originate in Latin roots and often represent abstractions rather than concrete things. Pile on too many, and your writing voice will fade out. Often you can find better options with fewer syllables. For example, consider the following pairs of words. Which do you prefer?

aviation or flight

consideration or thought

education or schooling

perambulation or walk

ramification or result

You may not have a choice. When writing about a chemical, you've got to use its name. But too often, we reach for a long word when a short one will do as well, if not better.

In the following exercises, you're going to explore the impact of word choice. As you work, analyze a variety of sources, including:

- Excerpts from your own writing

- Excerpts from various publications—ones you admire and those you find dull

- Pieces from writers whose voices you enjoy

You will identify words worth switching out. Then you'll hunt for replacements. I like to think of this as window shopping for words. It's fun and costs you nothing but time.

Use an online or print thesaurus when searching for replacements. You may see a lot of choices—heaps, bunches, a superabundance, a plenitude, or jillions of options. (Yes, I had fun with a thesaurus.) Which to choose? This week's exercises will help you identify candidates that have a positive impact on your writing voice.

Whittle Down the Weak Words

In this exercise, you're going to find opportunities to strengthen or refine your writing voice by replacing words that don't pull their weight.

Start by working with text you've written but haven't polished. Print it and pick up a highlighter. Find words you're willing to part with.

Candidates include:

- Words that appear too often

- Passive, lifeless verbs (like "is")

- Dull adjectives (*nice* and *big*)

- Words ending in *"tion"*

- Any others you sense aren't earning their keep.

Highlight the potential candidates. You may not replace them all, but you'll get a sense of the possibilities.

OBSERVATIONS

How many opportunities do you find for more interesting words? Even swapping one or two words can shift the writing voice.

Make a note of the top candidates in your own work by frequency.

1. _____

2. _____

3. _____

4. _____

Next, we'll go on a word shopping spree—starting in the "short word" department.

Swap In Shorter Words

Your first instinct may be to reach for impressive words to show readers how educated you are. If you want to cultivate an educated, expert voice, perhaps you think that a showy vocabulary is your path to glory.

Put that urge aside right now. Those long words may not make you appear as smart as you think. We know this thanks to Daniel Oppenheimer's wonderful study, "Consequences of Erudite Vernacular Utilized Irrespective of Necessity: Problems with Using Long Words Needlessly."[6] The study shows that elite words make people admire the writer *less*, not more.

Your goal is to fit your voice to the situation. Find words that sound great while carrying your message, and that keep the reader awake.

First, explore the unexpected power of short words. Short words affect the sound and rhythm, and keep the reader moving quickly.

Step 1: Your Own Work

Choose four or five potential candidates from the "weak words" list in the passage you used in the previous exercise or any particularly long words in your passage. For each, identify a shorter replacement—ideally one or two syllables. Or, use a phrase made up of short words to replace a longer word.

How does it read when you're done? Can you find shorter words that have an impact without making the writing sound too basic?

Track what you did and how it sounded below. Note the successful replacements, since you may want to use them in future revisions.

Original word: _____

Replacement: _____

Observation: _____

Original word: _____

Replacement: _____

Observation: _____

---

6 Oppenheimer's study was first published in *Applied Cognitive Psychology: The Official Journal of the Society for Applied Research in Memory and Cognition* in 2006. It won an Ig Nobel Prize in literature—an award celebrating the unusual and imaginative in science, medicine, and technology.

Original word: _____

Replacement: _____

Observation: _____

Original word: _____

Replacement: _____

Observation: _____

Step 2: Another Author's Work

Let's work with writing from an author who's no longer around to be offended. Here's a passage from Edgar Allan Poe's *Philosophy of Composition* in which he describes the process of composing *The Raven*.

> My next thought concerned the choice of an impression, or effect, to be conveyed: and here I may as well observe that, throughout the construction, I kept steadily in view the design of rendering the work *universally* appreciable. I should be carried too far out of my immediate topic were I to demonstrate a point upon which I have repeatedly insisted, and which, with the poetical, stands not in the slightest need of demonstration — the point, I mean, that Beauty is the sole legitimate province of the poem. A few words, however, in elucidation of my real meaning, which some of my friends have evinced a disposition to misrepresent.

I intend no disrespect to Poe. He wrote in a different era. The passage overflows with words that challenge modern readers, including many abstractions. Highlight a few of them. For example, look for the words ending in *"tion."*

Replace several candidates with shorter words. You may need to rework sentences entirely.

_____

_____

_____

_____

_____

_____

_____

_____

_____

_____

_____

_____

_____

_____

_____

_____

OBSERVATIONS

- Could you find words that fit the meaning as well, from your modern perspective?

- Do your replacements make the piece more meaningful to a modern ear?

- How do the edits affect the tone of Poe's voice?

Step 3: Write in Single Syllables

One holiday season, my family played a board game called "Poetry for Neanderthals." Like charades, players try to help teammates guess a word drawn from a stack of cards. A timer adds pressure.

Here's the catch: You give clues by speaking only one-syllable words.

It's harder than you think! If you accidentally say a two-syllable word, the opposing team hits you over the head with an inflatable club. That's the inspiration for this exercise. (No clubs needed.)

Can you possibly write with only single-syllable words, without sounding like Dr. Seuss or a Neanderthal? It can be done, but with care.

For example, consider another excerpt from Poe's essay cited above:

> My next thought concerned the choice of an impression, or effect, to be conveyed: and here I may as well observe that, throughout the construction, I kept steadily in view the design of rendering the work *universally* appreciable.

Here's one way to rewrite that with single-syllable words (unless you consider *poem* two syllables.)

> Next I thought of how the work would land, what state of mind it might bring forth. Here I should state that, as I wrote, I held this goal fast in my mind: a poem that pleased all who read it.

I tried to keep Poe's sentence constructions and nuanced thoughts. The result is not as poetic as Poe, but it does not sound like an early reader, either.

Work on a new piece using the following prompt. As you write, try to stick to one-syllable words as much as possible. (It's not always possible.) This may feel much harder than replacing longer words in an existing piece, since it constrains the Muse and slows down the flow. Alternatively, your Muse might enjoy the challenge!

Here's the prompt:

Describe your favorite place to write and why it inspires you.

_____

_____

_____

_____

_____

_____

_____

_____

_____

OBSERVATIONS

- What does the writing sound like when you do this? What happens to your voice?

  For example, does it sound:
  ☐ More serious
  ☐ Less serious
  ☐ Stronger
  ☐ Weaker
  ☐ Too simple
  ☐ More intimate
  ☐ Other: _____

- What is lost in sticking to single-syllable words? What is gained? Track your observations.

What is lost	What is gained

- Any other observations?

Look Around for Similar Sounds

When finding replacements, search out words that sound great with text already in the work. Search for:

- Alliteration (words that start with the same sound)

- Internal rhyme (words sharing similar sounds)

Even if you write serious nonfiction, small amounts of alliteration or internal rhyme delight the inner reading voice.

For example, the title of this chapter uses four words that begin with P: *Pick Words that Pack a Punch*. Does it seem like too much? I made that choice to communicate a playful tone. I hope you picked up on that, at least subconsciously.

Alliteration and internal rhymes please the inner reader by creating an audible, rhythmic pulse in the work. It can be quite subtle and may almost slip past you. Read this line from Chapter One of John Steinbeck's *Grapes of Wrath* aloud:

"In the water-cut gullies the earth dusted down in dry little streams."

Do you hear the rhythm of three words starting with *d* (dusted, down, dry)? The *d* sounds almost roll along the dusty streambed. It's subtle.

There's internal rhyme as well, which you may only detect when reading aloud. For example, listen to the repeated short *u* sound in *cut*, *gullies*, and *dusted*. This line is practically poetry.

Subtler still, read this sentence from the opening lines of *The Warmth of Other Suns* by Isabelle Wilkerson:

"The night clouds were closing in on the salt licks east of the oxbow lakes along the folds in the earth beyond the Yalobusha River."

You might not consciously notice *clouds/closing* as alliteration, nor the *licks/lakes* echo. Even the *-yond* and *Yalo-* echo each other. The sentence seems to sing and establishes a distinctive, finely tuned voice, appreciated by your inner reading voice.

Step 1: Finding Alliteration

Replace the following phrases with alliterative ones (both words starting with the same sound). You may choose to swap both words.

For example, if I want to replace the phrase *good writing*, I might start by searching for synonyms for various types of writing: prose, words, literature, books, blogs, essay, treatment, piece. Then, I'd use my ear to find interesting combinations: poetic prose, beautiful books, worthy words, exquisite exposition, fluent fiction ... You get the idea.

Forget about finding the "right" answer. Tune your ear to the power of alliteration and find the fun.

Large house: _____

Big tree: _____

Pretty flower: _____

Step 2: Add Alliteration to Your Own Work

Return to the writing sample in the first exercise, in which you highlighted words you might replace. This time, pick up the thesaurus and add alliteration to the sentence.

For example, let's say you want to replace "building understanding" in the following sentence:

> As a writer, you face a similar challenge <u>building understanding</u> in your reader's mind.

I might open a thesaurus and play with options:

> Creating comprehension (a little lengthy)

> Building belief (not quite right)

> Getting readers to grasp (ooh, I like grasp!)

Or, I could wipe out 'face a similar challenge" and cast a wider net:

> ... focus on fostering understanding ...

30

Try a few approaches. Write your winning combinations here:

1. _____

2. _____

3. _____

4. _____

5. _____

OBSERVATIONS

- Did you like any of the results?

- Was it fun?

Words That Create Character

A stage actor can broadcast a character with a few telling mannerisms. Colorful words have a similar effect on prose.

Ann Handley embodies this practice in her *Total Annarchy* newsletter, covering the intersection of marketing and writing. She drops unexpected words into the email greetings: *Hey, Sassafras! Hi, Tulip Bulb!*

In explaining this practice in the same newsletter, Ann writes,

> I toss an archaic or old-timey or unnecessarily long word like a hand grenade in the middle of a sentence. Harbinger. Nincompoop. Shenanigans. …Why? They're a little weird. We rarely use them in speaking. So they stand out. It's a stylistic choice I make.

Her loyal readers expect and enjoy this delightful expression of her personal voice.

Unusual words or phrases, used sparingly, make a distinct impression on the reader and contribute to how they perceive your voice. The English language is rife with words and expressions that linger on the fringes of everyday use.

The danger, of course, is that readers may not understand obscure words. As you experiment with the outliers, use them in context or otherwise make the meaning clear.

> **PRO TIP:** If you're ghostwriting for someone, read their work or listen to the way they speak to find their go-to phrases or words. Then add them to the writing like sprinkles on a cupcake. When people see their own words, they hear their own voice.

Step 1: Distinguish Tone and Sound

The following list includes pairs of words that appear on the same thesaurus page and thus overlap in meaning. Identify the "tone" or feeling you get from each.

Silliness: _____

Zaniness: _____

Know-how: _____

Sagaciousness: _____

Hindrance: _____

Glitch: _____

Deserted: _____

Forsaken: _____

OBSERVATIONS

- Did you notice the way the words sound? The *z* of *zaniness*, the *tch* of *glitch*? Use your ears to guide your choices.

Step 2: Choose an Outlier

Return to the first exercise in this chapter, *Whittle Down the Weak Words*. There, you highlighted words you might replace. This time, open your thesaurus and hunt for words that change the tone or character of the voice, if only for a moment.

For example, if I had written:

> As with almost anything in life, you'll improve with intentional practice.

Improve is a dull verb. I might choose words to adjust the tone:
- » *Make inroads* — more folksy
- » *Blossom* or *soar* — more inspiring
- » *Advance* — more formal

Rewrite your passage, adding a few outlier words that shift the tone to discover what minor changes can do.

_____

_____

_____

_____

_____

■■■ THIS WEEK:

READING: Pay attention to any unusual words you encounter in your reading. Make a list of words that make you smile or catch your attention.

WRITING: As you write, keep a thesaurus handy for word shopping. Challenge yourself to upgrade a word every day. Add an unusual word to your vocabulary or simply rekindle your love of the sound of words. Have fun!

■ ■ ■

WEEK 3

Track the Punctuation Prints

We often take punctuation for granted, thinking of it as a grammatical necessity rather than a meaningful part of our writing voices. Yet commas, colons, and dashes contribute in subtle ways to the writing voice.

Punctuation offers insight into the way the writer's or narrator's mind works.

For example, a semicolon signals a structured way of thinking. The em dash broadcasts a less formal mental connection—an interruption or a flash of insight. Punctuation contributes to the voice's confidence, formality, and even intimacy.

Most of all, punctuation creates the rhythm of the work, like the percussion section of a rock band.

- The hard stop of a period sounds final compared to the more nuanced "I'm not done yet" pause of a semicolon.

- The question mark creates pause and inflection, like a musical notation.

- Ellipses (...) telegraph a lingering, uncertain end rather than a hard stop— like a song that fades away.

In *Writing Tools*, Roy Peter Clark writes of punctuation as a kind of navigation or traffic control:

> If a period is a stop sign, then what kind of traffic flow is created by other marks? The comma is a speed bump; the semicolon is what a driver education teacher calls a "rolling stop"; the parenthetical expression is a detour; the colon is a flashing yellow light that announces something important up ahead; the dash is a tree branch in the road.

This week, we're going to look right past the words on the page to the punctuation. Bring your Scribe and a pen.

Writing Without Words

What happens if you strip out everything *except* the punctuation in your writing? It's like seeing the percussion line in an orchestral musical score—you can't tell the melody, but you get a sense of what's going on.

For example, here's a "punctuation print" of one of my blog posts:

,''!""?,,.'..(\',.)?',,,..',.,.,.?,.,.','',",.".·.?,.,,,,.',.
,.:..,,.,"'."(\','.)??.???:,,,,.,.',.,.?,.—..

Based on this, you might decide that my writing is fairly straightforward. The post poses a few questions and has fairly short, uncomplicated sentences, with a few parenthetical asides. Overall, it appears relatively restrained, except for that one exclamation point. (Hey, it's a blog post. It's allowed.)

Try the same thing with your own writing.

1. Pick a writing sample to examine. If possible, find a thousand or more words—a lengthy blog post, an email, or a chapter of a book you're working on. Longer is better.

2. Now capture *only* the punctuation marks—apostrophes, commas, everything that's not a word. You can do this by copying what you see or using an online tool.

My punctuation prints

_____

_____

OBSERVATIONS

- What do you notice about your punctuation? Are you a strict period-and-comma writer, or do you enjoy semicolons and parentheses?

- Do you use any specific punctuation marks more or less than you thought?

- What can you conclude about your writing voice based only on the punctuation? For example, strings of dashes or commas may indicate nuanced thoughts. Colons and semicolons tend to be more formal. What does your writing look like?

Compare Your Punctuation Across Formats

When I did that punctuation experiment on a chapter of one of my books, I found that my punctuation is *less* varied in books than in blog posts. I use fewer parenthetical asides. However, my emails and social media posts contain many more exclamation points. With less editing and revision, my thoughts range more freely and the punctuation reflects that.

How about you?

For this experiment, check the punctuation across the formats you work in. Just as you did in the previous exercise, extract only the punctuation. Here are a few suggestions; add the punctuation beneath the ones that apply to your writing life.

An email you send to a friend or family member

_____

A blog post

_____

A social media post

_____

A report for work

_____

A chapter of a book

_____

An essay

_____

Other:

_____

OBSERVATIONS

• Do the patterns shift as you switch formats? If so, how?

Peruse Other Writers' Punctuation

Some authors use punctuation in idiosyncratic ways, like Emily Dickinson and her dashes. And standards change over time. Today's writers would rarely punctuate the same way that Charles Dickens or Jane Austen did in the nineteenth century. It's fun to explore those differences.

Find authors whose style you admire. Just as you did in the previous experiments, strip out everything except punctuation from their work and compare them to yours.

For example, I compared my punctuation to a newsletter from the author George Saunders. His punctuation traces a nuanced thought structure, plus masterful use of language. It did not look like my straightforward blog post.

Here are a few ideas of pieces to examine. Go ahead and explore any of your favorite authors.

An article in today's news

_____

An article in a literary magazine

_____

A page from one of your favorite novels

_____

A page from a favorite nonfiction author

_____

Something else:

_____

OBSERVATIONS

• Does this exercise inspire you to play with punctuation as a factor of your voice?

■ ■ ■ **THIS WEEK:**

READING: Ponder the punctuation in blog posts, articles, and books. Note any personal, stylistic choices, and think about how they affect the sound and rhythm of the work, and the voice you perceive.

WRITING: Stretch your punctuation comfort zones. Experiment with a style of writing you rarely do, or back off a favorite punctuation mark. For example, if you are a huge fan of semicolons, experiment with the less formal em dash. If you love parenthetical asides, consider pulling a few of those ideas into their own sentences.

■ ■ ■

Find Your Sentence Rhythm

If the words are musical notes and punctuation percussion, sentences are the melodies that they create. This week, we're going to work with sentence length.

When working with nonfiction authors on their manuscripts, I often encourage people to break up blocks of longer sentences with a few shorter ones. This advice originates not from any bias for short sentences. I love long, lingering prose as much as the next person. No, I am concerned about the reader and the rhythm.

When nonfiction writers explain complicated topics, the writing mirrors the author's thought processes. Sentences string subordinate clauses together toward a satisfying resolution. Semicolons or dashes help the reader navigate with the author through the reasoning.

However, grammatical errors hide more easily in complex sentences. And even if you master every nuance of grammar and sentence construction, you risk overloading the reader's attention. Readers have to store parts of the sentence in working memory until they reach the end and assemble the meaning. After a while, that mental juggling becomes tiring.

Strings of long sentences create another reading hazard—they kill the rhythm of the work. Unless you are a masterful crafter of sentences, the work can become droning and tiring for the reader's inner reading voice.

Happily, you can reduce the rhythmic risk in a flash. Simply toss in an occasional short sentence to underscore an important point and give the reader's brain a moment to absorb ideas. In doing so, you'll change the rhythm.

Notice, please, that I don't suggest you write only in short sentences. Readers can become bored with short sentences unless the language is lovely or images powerful. Long sentences create their own rhythm—in the right hands, they are beautiful.

Read aloud this sentence from the opening paragraph of *The Lost Pianos of Siberia* by Sophy Roberts, describing a long train journey across Siberia.

> The train passes lazy trails of chimney smoke, gilded churches, and layers of snow stacked like bolts of silk, with the rhythm of the journey — the sluggish gait, the grinding stops into gaunt platforms and huddled towns — much as early travelers described Russian trains in the fashionable Siberian Railways sketches of the time.

The sentence is lengthy, layered with images and sounds like the railway journey itself. The next sentence, however, has two short sections: a beginning and an end.

> These days, however, fellow passengers are few; most Russians now fly to and from Siberia rather than use the railways.

The contrast in the sentence length and sound echoes the contrast between rail journeys and plane travel. The sentence structure reinforces the meaning.

We don't have to be as artistic as Roberts in this passage (although we can aspire to this height), but we can use sentence length to add texture and pacing to our work.

The Basic Sentence Exercise

Verlyn Klinkenborg is an author, former editor, and professor of writing at Yale University. He wrote an entire book with one sentence or clause per line: *Several Short Sentences About Writing*. It reads and looks like a prose poem.

Klinkenborg encourages his students to start with short, direct sentences. Doing so, they avoid the problem of overly long sentences, in which he laments, "the end of the sentence commonly forgets its beginning, as if the sentence were a long weary road to the wrong place."

His book inspired this exercise, which makes you consider the length of the sentences you use. Here it is:

1. Choose several paragraphs you've already written.

2. Reformat it or write it out again with one sentence per line.

If a long sentence doesn't fit on one line, let it wrap to the next. You want to see the pattern of short and long, making the rhythm visible. If you're using a computer, you can reduce the font size for the long ones.

Leave a blank line between paragraphs to show the structure.

One sentence per line

OBSERVATIONS

- What's the balance of long to short sentences in your work?

- Can you detect a rhythm in the sentences? Do you have a regular cadence of long to short (say, 2:1 or 3:1)?

- Break up a few of the long sentences, especially if they cluster together. Or, combine a couple of short sentences into a longer one. What does that do to the writing?

Scope Other Authors' Sentences

Find an author whose voice you admire and use the same technique on several paragraphs of their work, writing out one sentence per line to see the pattern.

Author/work: _____

_____

_____

_____

_____

_____

_____

_____

_____

_____

_____

_____

_____

_____

_____

OBSERVATIONS

- How does the sentence pattern for this author compare to your own writing in the last exercise? Does their cadence resemble yours?

- What would your work be like if you wrote in sentence patterns like theirs? Or would you even try?

Alternating Sentence Lengths

So far, we've been working with the Scribe, analyzing writing once it's done. Now let's bring the Muse to the table with new writing.

Using the same one-sentence-per-line strategy, alternate between short and long sentences while drafting. One short, one long, one short, etc.

Write a couple of paragraphs about your work in progress.

Or, use this writing prompt:

> *What's your writing goal for the next year? Looking back twelve months from now, what do you hope to say about the year?*

As you write, alternate sentence length. If your first sentence comes out long, the next must be short.

Here's how we'll define a "short" sentence:

- It has no parenthetical asides, dashes, or nested independent clauses (sentences within sentences).

- You can easily read it aloud, start to finish, without taking a breath.

- It fits on one line of the page. (No six-point font!)

In contrast, long sentences contain many words and perhaps multiple clauses. A long sentence should be a distinct contrast from its brief companions.

Use your judgment and ear. This exercise is about developing that ear.

New writing with alternating sentences

_____

_____

_____

_____

_____

_____

_____

_____

_____

_____

_____

_____

_____

_____

_____

_____

_____

_____

_____

_____

OBSERVATIONS

- How does alternating sentence length shape the experience of writing?

- How do you feel about the alternating balance?

- Did focusing on the sentence pattern make you more or less creative?

Your Ideal Sentence Ratio

When I shared this exercise with a group of writers, several came up with their own ratio of long-to-short sentences for the writing they did most frequently.

A few found the regular ratio of 2:1, or two long, one short. Others, three long, one short. Look at your own writing and what you learned from the previous exercise.

What ratio works best for you in your preferred writing format or genre?

- 1:1 Long to short

- 2:1 Long to short

- 3:1 Long to short

- 4:1 Long to short

- Other: _____

Do you change the pattern for different types of writing, such as a book manuscript compared to a blog post?

_____
_____
_____
_____
_____
_____
_____
_____
_____
_____
_____
_____
_____
_____

▪▪▪ THIS WEEK:

READING: When you find yourself enjoying written work, notice the sentence lengths. Conversely, if you're struggling through the prose, look at the sentences. Does the work have a pulse? Is it all long or all short?

WRITING: Experiment with breaking sentences up or gluing them together after you've written an email, blog post, or story. Listen to the rhythm as you do this.

▪ ▪ ▪

WEEK 5

Compose Paragraph Patterns

When you read your work aloud (as in Week 1), do you take an extra-long pause at the paragraph break?

Paragraph breaks treat the eyes, the ears, and the brain. The eyes enjoy white space because the page seems less daunting. The inner reader catches its breath. And the brain takes a moment to absorb the idea of the last paragraph before moving on to the next.

Many of us learned to write using an expository paragraph structure: a topic sentence, a few sentences with supporting details, and a conclusion or transition to the next paragraph. If you mastered this skill in school, good for you. But here's a question: How often do you write expository essays at work or for pleasure? Do you read them for fun?

Language is social, an ongoing improvisation and negotiation of meaning and expression. The rules of written language don't stay static as new types of writing proliferate. And as we spend more time reading online, on small screens designed to distract and tempt us elsewhere, reading itself is evolving.

As writers, we need to remember and account for those changes—even in decisions as simple as how we shape our paragraphs.

Many authors create manuscripts with monster paragraphs that occupy entire pages. And of course they do. That's what books have looked like for a long time. Pull older books from your bookshelf, or revisit classic novels. It's tempting to make your writing look the same, yet that decision might not serve your readers well.

Context matters. If we open a book and see pages filled with solid walls of text, with few paragraph breaks, we silently tell ourselves, "This is going to take focus." If we find the same wall of words online, we're likely to move on.

There are no hard-and-fast rules about paragraph length. As a useful guideline, try to restrain each paragraph to one major idea. Other than that, what you do depends on:

- What readers expect based on the format or medium: novel, memoir, non-fiction book, blog post, email, report, etc.

- The reader's available attention—how much focus are they likely to have for reading?

- The courage of your writing voice

What do I mean by "courage?" Do you have the skill to spin a pages-long paragraph, confident that your words will keep the reader enthralled? Do you have the courage to let a single, shining idea stand on its own, without being buttressed by supporting sentences?

You wouldn't want to write an entire book in one-sentence paragraphs, unless you made those sentences rich and varied. Otherwise, it may sound like an "early reader" book. But an occasional short paragraph might be welcome.

Many great writers know this and close their novels with a single-sentence paragraph. Read the end of *A Tale of Two Cities* by Charles Dickens:

> It is a far, far better thing that I do, than I have ever done; it is a far, far better rest that I go to than I have ever known.

This week, you'll explore how paragraph patterns affect voice.

Peruse Paragraph Patterns

We can measure paragraphs by sentences and by words. Both measures matter. Your Scribe will love this experiment, because it's time to gather data.

Pick four representative paragraphs from works you've written in your primary genre. For each paragraph, count the number of sentences and the total number of words. You'll work fastest by using the online word count capabilities in word processing software. But you can do it by hand, too.

After you've marked the four, calculate your average. (Add up the four entries and then divide by 4.)

Piece: _____

	Sentences	Words
Paragraph 1		
Paragraph 2		
Paragraph 3		
Paragraph 4		
Average Length		

Now you have a sense of *your* average paragraph lengths.

Next, find other authors you admire in your genre, and do the same thing for four paragraphs of their work:

Author and piece: _____

	Sentences	Words
Paragraph 1		
Paragraph 2		
Paragraph 3		
Paragraph 4		
Average Length		

How does your paragraph structure compare to theirs? Are yours longer in words or sentences? If you write short sentences, you may have more sentences but fewer words.

If you want to take this further, explore how paragraph lengths vary in specific media.

Article on the front page of a newspaper

Average length in sentences: _____

Average length in words: _____

Article in a popular magazine

Average length in sentences: _____

Average length in words: _____

Article in a literary magazine

Average length in sentences: _____

Average length in words: _____

Blog post by a writer you follow

Average length in sentences: _____

Average length in words: _____

OBSERVATIONS

- How does the paragraph length affect the overall tone of the writer's voice?

- Where does your writing fall in the pattern? It's okay to be an outlier—perhaps that's part of your voice.

Rearrange for Effect

The best way to grasp the impact of paragraphs is to play around with them. Experiment with how they stick together and what happens when you break one apart. Does it make a mess or does it shine light on a sentence that was otherwise crowded out?

Start by working with text you, personally, haven't written—you have less invested in it.

For your editing pleasure, here's a chunk of text from one of my books, with all paragraph breaks removed. (If you want to work with it online, you can find the text at AnneJanzer.com/Resources.)

> If you're writing about topics with a great deal of ambiguity, be prepared to encounter the already-made-up mind in your readers. The world is filled with complicated, ambiguous situations. It may take a while for the evidence to come in, or for a situation to clarify. During that transitional time, we either accept uncertainty or make provisional decisions. Some people find ambiguity inherently painful or difficult to handle, and seize on a quick decision. According to psychologist Arie Kruglanski, people exhibit different levels of a need for closure as a personality trait. Individual levels vary; you can take a quiz on Kruglanski's website to see where you land on his Need For Closure Scale. People with a strong need for closure tend to make decisions more quickly in uncertain situations. Having made a decision, they stick to it with more tenacity. And that tendency can lead them into trouble.

Allocate these sentences into paragraphs—as many or as few as you like. Rearrange the sentences if you want. Do this twice:

1. As a blog post for online reading. Remember that online readers need more white space.

2. As a section in a nonfiction book.

For each format, think about the following:

- The visual appearance of the page (particularly important for online reading)

- The rhythmic pulse of sentences and paragraphs (important for books)

- The distribution of meaning: do paragraphs deal with single ideas? Do you want to emphasize a point by putting it in its own paragraph?

Blog post

_____

_____

_____

_____

_____

_____

_____

_____

_____

Book excerpt

_____

_____

_____

_____

_____

_____

_____

_____

_____

OBSERVATIONS

- Did you make the same decisions for each format?

- Did you change the cadence of long-to-short paragraphs as you switched formats?

- Do you have any other observations to track about using paragraphs?

 » _____

    _____

 » _____

    _____

 » _____

    _____

Write to a Paragraph Pattern

Now it's time to infuse paragraph patterns into the act of drafting, to see how it affects your writing voice. Let's bring your Muse into the work.

As you draft, write in a pattern of long and short paragraphs. It may feel awkward. In real life, you rarely need to write in an artificial rhythm like this. But this exercise entices the Muse to consider the sound or visual impact of paragraph breaks.

1. Choose a format for the work. Are you writing a book excerpt? A blog post?

2. Pick a paragraph pattern you'd like to match. Use one of the following patterns, if you're not sure.

• Blog post: 1 long, 1 short

• Book: 2 or 3 long, 1 short

• Other: _____

Now write several paragraphs. You can write on a subject already at hand, or use this prompt:

Write about a time you took a creative risk that paid off.

Paragraph pattern exercise

_____

_____

_____

_____

_____

_____

_____

_____

_____

_____

■ ■ ■ THIS WEEK:

READING: Pay attention to paragraphs in your reading. Does the paragraph pattern shift between publications and types of work? Do you spot consistent patterns in the works of specific authors?

WRITING: Experiment with lengthening a few paragraphs and shortening others. How does it affect your writing voice?

■ ■ ■

WEEK 6

Readability

Everyone likes to make fun of impenetrable academic writing. Academic settings inspire a kind of verbal escalation. Students arrive feeling the pressure to write at a "college level," whatever that means. So they perfect long, wandering sentences filled with scholarly vocabulary. The prose may reach a point at which only the author understands what they were trying to express.

Ironically, in reaching for an elevated, erudite tone, we do ourselves a disservice. Remember the study cited in Week 2, "Consequences of erudite vernacular utilized irrespective of necessity: Problems with using long words needlessly." We do not appear smarter when pulling out the long words. In reaching for an advanced reading level, we often overreach ourselves.

(Note to college students: If you can express college-level concepts at an eighth-grade reading level, you will quickly become a grader's favorite.)

Great nonfiction writers teach us that we can write about complicated, abstract topics without dense prose. Read any of Michael Lewis' books about finance. The concepts may be gnarly, but the words flow.

According to the Center for Plain Language, the average American reads at a seventh- to eighth-grade level. Even if you write for highly educated readers, consider their context. How stressful or busy is their day? Are you writing in their native language, or do they have to translate as they read? At the end of a day filled with a mountain of content, your readers may not welcome college-level prose.

This week, we're going to experiment with readability. What kind of education, familiarity with language, or level of focused attention do you ask of the reader who is your necessary companion and the ultimate judge of your success? What "reading level" do you write for?

Most readability scores or reading levels are measured using the Flesch Reading Ease calculation. This score involves only two key variables:

1. Average number of syllables in a word

2. Average number of words in a sentence

That's it, nothing more. This surprised me—I thought it was more complicated.

Of course, Flesch Reading Ease can't perfectly determine reading level. You could write impenetrable prose with short sentences and words. (Hmm, that would be a fun challenge.)

However, everyone uses the calculation and it's good enough. So, play with it. You've already experimented with both word length and sentence length. You have everything you need to hack your readability scores.

Check Your Readability Level

For this experiment, you need text you've written and a way to measure the reading level. You can find readability tools in many places:

- In Microsoft Word, find it in the Spelling and Grammar editor.

- Tools like Grammarly or ProWritingAid (look for Readability)

- Online calculators. Search for "Flesch Kincaid calculator" to see a few options. Then cut and paste your work into the site.

Some tools report the Readability Score on a scale of 1 to 100—higher is easier to read. Others report the Reading Level—higher is harder to read. And a few tools give you both.

Before you start, take your best guess at the reading level of your writing. Then, use a calculator to check the score or grade level.

OBSERVATIONS

- Initial guess: I think I write at this relative grade level: _____

- What's the Readability score (1 to 100) of your writing _____

- What's the Reading Level (usually expressed as a grade)?_____

- Is it lower or higher than expected? _____

- Is this a surprise? Why, or why not? _____

_____

_____

- Are you happy with it? _____

OTHER OBSERVATIONS

_____

_____

_____

_____

Make It More Readable

If the reading level was higher than eighth grade or the Readability score lower than 70, try to make your writing more accessible according to the algorithms.

- Shorten sentences

- Swap in shorter words.

Run it through the calculator and see if it made a difference.

Starting level: _____

Ending level: _____

OBSERVATIONS

- How easy is it to increase readability?

- Did you like the resulting text better?

- What did you learn…

About sentence length? _____

About word length? _____

Make Your Work *Less* Readable

Next, try making the work less readable—for fun, if nothing else.

Go ahead, embellish the prose. Combine a few sentences into longer ones. Swap in lengthier words. Dust off the vocabulary you learned in school or think of the most obscure industry terms you know.

You can take this experiment to extremes. I tried to make one of my blog posts read at a twelfth grade level and nearly self-destructed.

Track how you did:

Starting level: _____

Ending level: _____

OBSERVATIONS

- How hard was it to make your writing *less* readable?

- What do you think about the result?

- Did it make you seem "smarter" on the page? Or, did it make you sound more distant or overly academic?

- What else happened to your writing voice?

- Any other observations?

_____

_____

_____

_____

_____

Check Other Writers' Readability

Now that you've played with the readability of your own writing, calculate the scores for other pieces.

Here are a few examples to plug into a readability calculator:

- Today's front-page news article

- A blog post or LinkedIn article by a favorite writer

- Technical instructions

- A legal document

- A book chapter or short story by an author you admire (this is easiest if you have an online source)

For each piece, first *guess* the Reading Level or Readability score (Use whichever score you find most comfortable.) Then, run it through and check the results.

Piece	Readability guess	Actual score

OBSERVATIONS

- How accurate were your guesses? What did you base them on?

- What did you learn about your favorite writers or writing sources?

- How did those Readability Scores compare to yours?

- Did any of them surprise you? If so, why?

■ ■ ■ THIS WEEK:

READING: As you encounter works you enjoy reading, check their Reading Levels. Pay attention to anything that surprises you.

WRITING: Think about where you want your work to land on these scales. Experiment with writing at harder or easier reading levels, just for the fun of it. You may find that you enjoy working in slightly different territories.

■ ■ ■

WEEK 7

State Your Intentions

So far, we've been looking at writing on the page. Your Scribe may have enjoyed this work. For the next six weeks, we dive into your mind, because ultimately the writing voice expresses human thought, emotions, and personality.

Think about why you write and who you serve. It's time to state your intentions.

Each of us writes for many reasons. Other than personal journals, we write because we intend other people to read, and for the words to affect them. We might hope to entertain, educate, inspire, or persuade others. Those goals influence our voices.

Without clear goals, the writing voice may be muddy. And if we're not open or honest in our intentions, the reader will add their own.

People I don't know often send me emails or LinkedIn messages claiming their desire to help me with my website or books, while urging me to schedule a call with them or post their blog on my site. If I interpreted their words literally, I would think the world was full of helpful strangers. Perhaps some of them are. But behind the words I sense their stronger motivation for a sale, a backlink, whatever.

Our underlying intentions seep through the words.

We may have many reasons for writing, and of course they include self-serving goals. When I surveyed more than 400 nonfiction authors about why they wrote books, many indicated personal reasons: writing a book had been a lifelong ambition, or they wanted to accomplish a major project like a book. Many listed business objectives—writing a book helps a speaker's career, for example. A scant 2 percent hoped for "fame and fortune."[7]

---

7 Find the results of the nonfiction author survey at https://annejanzer.com/nonfiction-authors/

Eighty percent of the authors selected the following statement as one of their reasons: "I want to serve others with what I know." We are driven by a sense of purpose.

Remember that ultimately, readers decide whether or not your writing works. If you focus on serving them with your words, your chances of success increase. Let's call this philosophy *servant authorship*—writing to serve specific people with your ideas. It can be a powerful motivator.

Who do you serve, and what do they need?[8]

Returning to this simple question guides you through many dilemmas with your work, including questions about voice.

For example, should you be authoritative or companionable? Should you write with humor and levity, or absolute clarity? What voice does your reader need or want for the piece you are writing?

Sure, you want to write in a voice that seems authentic. You want to match that authentic part of yourself with the purpose of the piece. As you tinker with voice, consider your readers' expectations and needs. For example:

- Is the topic stressful to them—and can you mitigate that stress or anxiety? Perhaps they need expert reassurance.

- Are they curious about the subject or do you need to spark their curiosity and win them over? Your voice may need to be compelling, entertaining, or companionable.

- Will they read this as part of a long, dull day swamped with constant demands on their attention? Can you offer a moment of relief? Perhaps they need a light and playful voice from you.

Servant authorship clearly applies to nonfiction. For example, if you write text guiding people through a complicated and stressful situation, your readers may need both clarity and reassurance or compassion. If your voice embodies those attributes, people are more likely to absorb your ideas.

All writing serves its readers—fiction, poetry, essay, and business documents. Why will a reader pick up your book or story? Why will they spend time with your poem? For escapism? To learn something? For insight into the human condition? A combination of those things?

The experiments that follow dig further into the idea of servant authorship.

---

8 I realize that "whom" is grammatically correct. To my ear, that makes my voice sound stuffier than I am!

The first asks you to explore what servant authorship means in your work by identifying the readers you serve, your intention for them, and what they need from you. This may be the single most important exercise in this book. It applies well to any writing project you do, and could legitimately become part of your ongoing writing practice.

Who Do You Serve and How?

Choose one specific project: a blog post, a book, an email, a poem, a report, or anything else.

Answer the following questions about this project:

1. Who do you hope to serve? (This might be an individual or distinct group.)

2. What do you intend for them to get from the work? Why will they read it?

3. What do they need from you?

Choosing an audience or group of readers stumps many writers. At times, you know precisely who will read your work. More often, you aren't sure. That's okay.

Identify a group you *hope* to reach. You don't have to know their demographics (age, income, where they live). Instead, think about their internal landscape—what do they want? What might lead them to peruse what you have written, whether it's a blog post or a report?

If you're writing a cozy mystery, you might focus on readers who love a specific author you match well with, or who want to lose themselves in a personality-based puzzle. Perhaps your setting will draw a specific set of readers, such as people who like stories set in the Arctic.

If your work reaches multiple audiences, you might run through the questions a few times, answering them for each group. If those groups of readers have conflicting needs, decide which set of readers to prioritize. It's better to serve one group very well than all groups poorly.

Once you have identified the group, state your intentions for them through the work, and think about what they need from you.

Try it now, with one piece of writing and one specific audience. This exercise may require time and thought. When we write, we're so deeply inside our own heads that it's hard to flip the switch and think from the reader's perspective. Doing so will make you a more empathetic and effective writer.

Servant authorship statement for _____

Reader group
Name *one* distinct group of people you hope to serve with your writing. (If there are several, choose one.)

_____

Your intention for them
What do you hope they will get from reading it? (Entertainment? A fresh perspective? Useful knowledge?)

_____

What they need from you
What do they need from you for that to happen? Pick all that apply:

- ☐ Clear, specific instructions

- ☐ Confirming data

- ☐ Stories

- ☐ Background data and explanations

- ☐ Confidence or reassurance

- ☐ Memorable, pithy phrases

- ☐ Humor

- ☐ Poetic prose

- ☐ Other: _____

Do you have more than one set of reader profiles for the same writing project? Answer the same questions again for a different group:

Reader group

_____

Your intention for them

_____

What they need from you

- ☐ Clear, specific instructions
- ☐ Confirming data
- ☐ Stories
- ☐ Background data and explanations
- ☐ Confidence or reassurance
- ☐ Memorable, pithy phrases
- ☐ Humor
- ☐ Poetic prose
- ☐ Other: _____

OBSERVATIONS

- How hard was it to fill this out?

- Did the servant authorship statement clarify your thoughts on the writing project?

- What does this tell you about how to tailor your writing voice?

Inform, Persuade, Entertain

Let's dig deeper into your intentions. People often suggest that writing serves one of three purposes: *inform, persuade,* or *entertain.* These categories cover a wide range. Your own goals may be quite specific:

1. Inspire people to be kind to one another

2. Comfort people in a time of grief

3. Offer an escape into another world that gives readers perspective on their own

You don't need to choose a single goal: most good writing works at multiple levels. For example, your primary goal may be informing people, but if they also enjoy reading, they are more likely to learn. Perhaps you write humor and want to make people laugh, and then think.

In this exercise, you're going to bypass your primary intention and focus entirely on a secondary one.

Let's say I wanted to describe how to tie a shoe (informative) in a poetic voice (entertaining). By focusing exclusively on being poetic rather than informative, I write this:

> The trail calls, you must answer. Prepare yourself with an open gaze, a sturdy stick, and shoes that connect you with the earth. Gather the loose ends of your shoelaces, as you collect your untethered thoughts and focus on the trail. Bind the shoe firmly to your foot by intertwining those laces—right over left, then around and underneath. Feel the embrace of the shoe becoming one with your foot in movement and intention. This first knot is flimsy and fleeting. Like resolutions, it needs reinforcement, with a second knot of loops.

I may have shot right past *poetic* to *pathetic.* That's fine, I was experimenting. I had fun writing this, as I rarely do anything like it.

Choose a subject to write about and identify its primary intention. You can work with one of the following prompts (each identified by a primary intention):

Inform: *How to gift-wrap a book*

Persuade: *Encourage the reader to come to your book signing/meeting*

Entertain: *Describe the clouds in the sky*

Now write several sentences on the topic, focusing on a *different* intention. For example, write a persuasive piece about the clouds in the sky, or an entertaining piece about gift-wrapping a book.

_____

_____

_____

_____

_____

_____

_____

_____

_____

_____

_____

_____

OBSERVATIONS

- What does it feel like to work against the usual intention?

- How did you change your writing voice when choosing a different intention?
    - ☐ Elevate the prose
    - ☐ Add stories
    - ☐ Use different pronouns (I, me, you, etc.)
    - ☐ Add more description
    - ☐ Use longer sentences
    - ☐ Use shorter sentences
    - ☐ Shift from your usual punctuation
    - ☐ Other: _____

- What does this teach you about the way you naturally approach subjects?

- Do you want to keep any of these techniques? Which ones?

_____

- What's the primary intention for most of your writing? The secondary? Number 1 for primary, 2 for secondary:

Inform _____

Persuade _____

Entertain _____

Other: _____

Letter to the Author

The third servant authorship question asks what our readers need from us. We come to our work full of our own objectives. What we want and what readers need are not always a perfect match.

This experiment exercises *cognitive empathy*, or understanding what another person might think or feel. I use it when I'm stuck or uncertain. And it certainly applies to finding the right voice.

Think of a current writing project you're working on or plan to undertake. It could be anything from a poem to a blog post or an email to your manager. Pick one person you want to reach.

Now write yourself (the writer) a letter from that reader's perspective, all about that topic. Have them tell you what frustrates them or what they have heard but may not understand. Use this exercise to mine any preconceptions readers may bring to the subject, or to explore what they want the experience of reading to be like.

Put it all in your reader's voice.

For example, if I were doing this exercise, I would write myself a note from an imagined reader of this book:

> Dear Anne,
>
> I am not entirely happy with the way I show up when I write. It sounds boring and corporate. And I'm *not* a boring person! I've read so much about finding an "authentic" voice, but what is that, and how do I know when I have it? Does that imply that everything I write needs to be *conversational*? What if I want to show up as authoritative at work? Should I write more forcefully than I would speak? And what does all of this mean for the novel I'm writing in my spare time?
>
> Yours,
> *Confused*

Try it yourself.

Letter from my reader:

Dear _____ (your name)

_____

_____

_____

_____

_____

_____

_____

_____

_____

_____

_____

_____

OBSERVATION

- Did this exercise clarify anything about your project?

- What (if anything) did you discover about your readers' wants, needs, and fears?

  Wants: _____

  _____

  Needs: _____

  _____

  Fears: _____

  _____

If you were writing directly back to the writer in response, what would your voice sound like? Should you bring that into the work itself?

■ ■ ■ **THIS WEEK:**

READING: As you read, can you identify the writer's intentions for you? Do you sense that they're thinking of you at all?

WRITING: Before you write anything, even an email, run through the three servant authorship questions: Who am I writing for, what do I intend for them, and what do they need? Although it may seem to add more time to your writing process, doing this usually makes the work better and often generates ideas.

■ ■ ■

WEEK 8

You as a Fictional Character

In December 2022, the *New York Times* challenged several children's authors and writing teachers to identify whether ChatGPT or human fourth-graders wrote a collection of essays.[9]

The experts could not always tell the difference. Nor could I. Many of us find that unsettling.

When we read, we form an image of the narrator as a human being. With good fiction, characters come to life in our heads. Even when we encounter writing from a "brand" or a chatbot, it's hard to resist giving it a personality. (I thank automated help chatbots when they answer my questions.)

Your readers probably don't know you personally. As they read your words, they interpret your voice and create an idea of the person writing those words. They construct an image of you that is, in a sense, a fictional character.

Even the most dedicated journalists, memoirists, and professional writers engage in a type of fiction: the way they portray themselves in print. When we write in our own voice, we present a curated version of ourselves. The complete self would never fit.

We do this almost without thinking. In my survey about writing voice, two-thirds of respondents reported writing in a professional voice for a portion of their work. No doubt they sound different when writing fiction, personal essays, journals, and emails to friends and family.

---

9 The article about ChatGPT emulating fourth-graders appeared in the December 26 edition of the *New York Times*. Read it yourself and see if you can figure out which samples represent real children, and which are AI.

What happens if we think of ourselves as fictional characters—even if we write nonfiction? Could this increase the fluidity of our writing? That's what we're going to explore this week.

Sketch Your Character

In this exercise, you're going to sketch a brief character profile of the narrator (which may be you) *as that persona relates to the work at hand.*

- If you write in your own voice, remember that you present only a specific slice of yourself on the page—the one the reader needs.

- If you write fiction with an omniscient narrator, that persona still has a point of reference, a lens on the world, and a distinct voice.

How about memoir? Isn't that really you on the page? Yes, although it represents you at a specific time of life. So, draw a quick character profile of yourself at that time, as related to your memoir's theme. Your entire life won't fit.

Draft a short profile of the narrator in the third person.

This isn't the bio that would appear on a book jacket, filled with your credentials—leave that for another time. You're trying to capture the personality you hope to project in the writing voice. You can do that in a few short paragraphs.

Keep the writing in the third person so you can zoom out and get perspective.

For example, here's a profile I might write for myself as the narrator of this workbook.

> Anne is an author who stumbled into writing books after years of writing for companies. She'd spent many years as a freelance marketer, shifting her writing voice to sound like this brand or that corporate executive. Over time, she realized that she could select a voice each time she writes, even in her own name.
>
> Now she researches and writes about topics of her own choosing—a prospect that both terrifies and delights her. Feeling the weight of responsibility to write something worth the time and effort of reading, she probably does too much research. She takes great joy in language and hopes to help others find similar pleasure.

These are the parts of myself that seem relevant to who I am as author of this book. I could have gone on about other details—my first dog was a beagle, I'm the youngest of four, we had writers in the family, and so on. Those aspects of my life don't matter here, not for a workbook. You only need to know about me as a companion or guide on this journey.

Remember, as with all the exercises here, you don't have to show this to anyone.

Your narrator profile:

_____

_____

_____

_____

_____

_____

_____

_____

_____

_____

_____

_____

_____

_____

_____

_____

_____

_____

_____

_____

_____

_____

OBSERVATIONS

- What can you do with the insights from this exercise?

- What would a reader know, or guess, about you by reading the work alone, without the bio?

- Does this bio shape your ideas about what your writing voice should sound like? If so, how?

  » My voice could be more _____

  » My voice could be less _____

Pick Three Adjectives

Here's a useful marketing trick. Pick three adjectives that you would like to embody in your writing. They can be anything: smart, expert, funny, compassionate, nerdy, whatever. The options are nearly infinite—and that's the fun of it.

You can only claim three, so choose carefully. You'll be lucky to communicate two consistently.

> **PRO TIP:** When you're ghostwriting or writing in a brand voice, ask for these three adjectives before you start. It will save everyone time.

My three adjectives:

1. _____

2. _____

3. _____

Now choose one of your adjectives and take it to an absurd extreme. For example, one of my adjectives is *curious*. If I went overboard, I might write an email like this to friends:

> Remember that we're getting together Saturday for wine tasting at 6pm at Pat's place. I wonder what wines everyone will bring—and if there are any great tasters in our midst. I read a book by a Master Sommelier, and it includes a tasting grid. Does anyone want to try it with me? Maybe we should make it a blind tasting and see how our different senses compare. Is anyone planning to spit out the wine? And what's the best food to accompany wine tasting? I'll do some research and bring a snack that works well.

(See how annoying it can be to go too far?)

Try "going overboard" with one of your own adjectives. Either write a paragraph or two on a current project or use the following prompt:

Write an email to friends about a gathering on Saturday.

Adjective: _____

Sample:

_____

_____

_____

_____

_____

_____

_____

_____

_____

_____

_____

_____

_____

_____

_____

_____

_____

_____

_____

_____

Try On Another Character

Pick a favorite fictional character—one you know well and that you can inhabit easily.

Choose characters with distinct voices. For example, if you love reading mysteries, pick your favorite sleuth or detective: Hercule Poirot, Sam Spade. Consider any of the Harry Potter characters. Or, try on a movie character.

Put them to work writing for you. How would Snape write that email? How would Yoda begin your blog post?

For example, I tried asking Poirot to describe my favorite hike, and he just complained about his shoes and the lack of a tisane.

If you don't have a writing project in mind, use this prompt:

> *Write about a specific place you love from the perspective of your chosen character, who may or may not love it.*

Character: _____

Topic: _____

_____

_____

_____

_____

_____

_____

_____

_____

_____

_____

_____

_____

OBSERVATIONS

- How was that experience? Was it fun to write in an unfamiliar voice?

- Did writing as another character shift your perspective? For example, if you used the prompt, did it make you consider the place again through a new lens?

- Are there elements of that character's voice you might call on in the future? If so, what are they?

_____

- I am like _____ [the character] in these ways:

  » _____

  » _____

  » _____

- I am different from _____ in these ways:

  » _____

  » _____

  » _____

■ ■ ■ THIS WEEK:

READING: Notice the impressions you form of the author when you read. Do you hear individual journalists' voices when reading the news? Do you detect the person behind a business report, the narrator's voice in the novel, the poet's voice in a poem? Pay attention to whether and how you instinctively sketch the characters.

WRITING: As you write, think about how you want to show up as a character. Return to your servant authorship exercise in Week 7 and ask: How does the reader need or want me to appear?

■ ■ ■

WEEK 9

Presence or Absence

"Call me Ishmael."

The narrator of Herman Melville's *Moby-Dick* begins the book by introducing himself. He declares his presence and tells his story, taking his place alongside us, the readers.

Now consider a textbook, perhaps one written by a team of authors. Or, look at a front-page news item from a reputable newspaper. The writer or narrator seems absent, hidden behind the curtain.

Everything we write has an implied narrator producing the words. As readers, we construct the persona of the narrator as we read. It's impossible to be entirely absent from our writing. Even the intentionally distant journalist, without a byline, inhabits the voice of the publication they represent. The marketer writes with the voice of a brand.

How present are you as the writer or narrator in your work?

Your decision depends on context and genre. For personal essays, memoir, or travel writing, you tell stories from your experience. You may choose first-person pronouns, like *I* and *we*. Being fully present, you claim a relationship with the reader, as Ishmael does.

If you write operational reports, technical instructions, history books, or marketing copy, you may choose instead to disappear and keep the spotlight on the content. But make no mistake, the reader still forms an impression of the narrator, consciously or not.

Fiction writers dance with this dilemma as well. A third-person *omniscient* narrator (a voice that knows what's going on in people's heads) exhibits a perspective.

The narrator holds up the lens for the reader to look through, and thus is present in an indirect sense. Jane Austen's third-person narrator has a clear point of view and sense of humor that we attribute to the author herself.

Think of presence and absence as a gradient. Most writing falls not quite at either extreme.

We get comfortable with the way we've always written, whether personal and confessional, distant, or in between. This week, you're going to experiment with writing outside your usual patterns and discovering what that does to your writing voice.

Disappear Entirely

These first two experiments explore extremes of the presence spectrum: the visible narrator versus the invisible one.

Pick a short passage of your own that represents the work you want to do. Or, try this prompt, writing about it in your default writing voice:

Describe the trees or plants that grow near you, and how they contribute to the "sense of place" or feeling of the area.

First, assess how present you are in the work as written, on a scale of 1 (completely absent or not there) to 5 (completely visible). For example, a "Do not park" sign is a 1 and a personal story is a 5.

	1	2	3	4	5	
Absent	○	○	○	○	○	Present

If you were already at a 1 (not present at all), skip to the next exercise.

Otherwise, rewrite the passage to remove all traces of you, the author or narrator. The word *I* should never appear. No humorous asides. Try to sound like a bot—and not a good one. If you must appear, write about yourself in the third person, as "the author."

Have fun. Don't be harsh with yourself. You're playing with the extremes, and the results *should* be awful. That's what makes it fun.

Completely Absent Narrator Passage

OBSERVATIONS

- Read it when you're done. Does it sound like you?

- Does it have a different mood or voice?

- Was it easy or hard to remove yourself?

Be Too Intrusive

Now rewrite that same passage so that you are intrusively present. Insert yourself into nearly every sentence, whether or not it makes sense.

Make everything about your own opinion, your personal experiences, your impressions. Go much farther than you would show anyone. We learn by testing the extremes.

Completely Visible Narrator Passage

_____

_____

_____

_____

_____

_____

_____

_____

_____

OBSERVATIONS

• Which was easier, being overly absent or overly present?

• What does this tell you about the way you normally write?

• Can you detect how the reader might perceive you when reading these opposing options?

• On the 1-to-5 spectrum of absent to present, where does your writing usually fall?

	1	2	3	4	5	
Absent	○	○	○	○	○	Present

• Would you like to nudge it in another direction? Why?

Violate Expectations

Just for fun, see what happens if you do the *opposite* of what the reader expects for a specific type of writing.

Write a series of text messages or an email to a family member without appearing yourself. Be absent. (Don't send it, though, or you may damage the relationship!)

_____

_____

_____

_____

_____

_____

Write a "No Parking" notice in a completely visible way, inserting yourself. Showing up when you're not expected can be fun!

_____

_____

_____

_____

_____

_____

OBSERVATIONS

- Does this exercise inspire you to experiment with other ways of showing up in your work?

- Does it offer fresh perspective on your voice?

■ ■ ■ THIS WEEK:

READING: Identify where the articles, books, reports, and blog posts you read fall on the 1-5 presence scale.

> 1: Completely absent

> 5: Entirely present

> Notice when something doesn't match your expectations for a genre, and what effect that has on you.

WRITING: Before writing, decide explicitly how present you want to be. Choose a number on the scale and experiment with it. Test whether this changes your approach to your voice.

■ ■ ■

WEEK 10

Relating to the Reader

We usually know who's calling when we answer a phone. When I see a friend's name, I answer cheerfully: "Hey there!" If it's the dentist's office, I'm polite and friendly. And if there's no name attached, I am both cautious and noncommittal — *if* I answer at all.

In the few seconds it takes to pick up the phone, we adjust our speaking voice based on our relationship to the other party. This happens almost unconsciously. The same can happen when we pick up a pen or put our hands on the keyboard.

You've probably heard the advice to picture your reader. I hope that the servant authorship exercise in Week 7 helped you think about people you want to reach. That's only the first step.

Once you have a reader in mind, decide the relationship you hope to establish with them. Are you a guide or a companion? A friendly voice or a distant, formal one?

Your decision will connect to last week's theme of presence or absence. It's hard for an absent narrator to create a close, companionable relationship with the reader.

Remember that the reader interprets your writing voice, in part based on their perceived connection with you. If you don't establish and nurture that relationship with care, you may find that your writing exhibits a voice you don't intend.

Formal, Informal, Intimate, or Distant

Whether you write in your name or that of a fictional character or business brand, the formality of the tone creates the foundation of your voice.

Do you use elevated language or everyday prose? Most of us have a natural speaking register and can pitch our voices higher or lower as needed. The same is true for writing.

- In writing, a high register projects an elevated, educated tone with more ornate sentences and refined word choices. Well-written prose in a high register can be a joy to read. Poorly written, it's a brutal slog.

- The low register represents the most accessible type of language. It may operate in idioms and play fast and loose with grammar. *You get my drift?*

Where does your writing fall on this spectrum?

There's no single, correct answer. Your voice undoubtedly shifts according to the medium. An overly familiar tone might offend readers in certain cultures. Genres bring expectations as well. A legal notice is usually formal.

Most of us live our writing and reading lives in the middle, between the extremes of high and low. Well-written middle register prose is straightforward and effective. (This book falls into this middle ground most of the time, although it tips to informal. That's an intentional choice.)

You can approach the formal/informal spectrum in several ways:

- Polite to familiar

- Reverent to irreverent

- Erudite to plainspoken (high to low register)

This week's experiments deal with various aspects of the writer/reader connection. You'll play with extremes of pronoun usage, high and low voice, and distance or companionship.

Getting Personal with Pronouns

Working with pronouns is one of the quickest ways to establish the relationship with the reader.

- The pronouns *you* and *we* shorten the distance between the narrator and the reader.

- Using *we* and *us* aligns yourself with the reader, claiming a closer connection.

- Using *one* instead of *you* creates more distance.

Often, pronoun decisions come down to personal style or the conventions of your genre. You may even establish a habit. But don't get too comfortable with your choices. Use the right pronoun (or noun) for the job.

When writing about difficult situations, maintaining distance helps readers feel less defensive or negative. For example, consider this passage about Imposter Syndrome:

> When you have Imposter Syndrome, you believe at some level that you're not a real writer.

If the reader is vulnerable to Imposter Syndrome (and who isn't?), they might feel uncomfortable with the second person pronoun, *you*. Hearing themselves addressed directly might lead them to experience Imposter Syndrome once again. Switching the subject offers perspective on their situation without triggering the emotion.

> When people experience Imposter Syndrome, they believe at some level that they're not real writers.

Do you notice the subtle difference? When reading that passage, the reader now considers themselves a member of a large group of people who experience the situation. They might be more open to solutions when taking this broader perspective.

Experiment with playing against expectations with pronouns. Remove the personal pronouns when you would normally use them or add them when they aren't expected.

Write a short message (like a text message) to a family member, inviting them over for a holiday, but avoid all personal pronouns (*you, me/I, we/us, they*). Then, write a "Stay on the Trails" sign for a local park, using the personal pronouns *you* and *I* or *we*.

Text message invitation without personal pronouns

_____

_____

"Stay on the Trails" sign with personal pronouns

_____

_____

OBSERVATIONS

- Which message seems more welcoming: the invitation or the sign?

  ☐ Invitation

  ☐ Sign

- Which type of writing felt more familiar to you?

- If you never use personal pronouns in your writing, would you consider it? (Personal pronouns are becoming more accepted in business writing, by the way.)

- If you always use personal pronouns, are there places you might dial them back?

Fancy or Folksy

For this exercise, we're going to experiment with one aspect of formality: are you fancy or folksy?

Fancy, in this case, means using the high register: elevated language, with ornate sentences and advanced vocabulary, formal punctuation, and few contractions. A folksy narrator uses basic vocabulary and grammar, and may include idioms and slang.

The exercise below asks you to write at both ends of the spectrum. By taking things to absurd extremes, we learn about what is comfortable while pushing our limits.

For inspiration, here's a description of how to tie a shoe in pseudo-legalese (a very specific kind of elevated voice):

> Inasmuch as it is the obligation of a citizen to traverse common, public spaces without imperiling others or imposing undue liability on property owners, every person wearing footwear designed to be held on the foot by adjustable laces (excluding previously tied laces sewn on and held with elastic) shall fasten the two ends of the laces together in a form that keeps the shoe on the foot without creating a tripping hazard (and thus presenting questions of subsequent liability) for the wearer and those around them. The commonly accepted method of arranging these ties consists of two phases: 1) an initial half knot to set the desired degree of snugness, followed by 2) arranging the loose ends of the ties in a two-loop bow to safely secure the first knot while gathering the excess laces into the area above the wearer's foot, using the technique described in the "Bunny Ears" rhyme (copyright unknown). In certain situations, such as extra-long or slippery laces, wearers may add a third half-knot using the two loops of the bow. This procedure, sometimes referred to as "double-knotting," adds a degree of security while in transit, but entails extra work when commencing and ending the duration of the shoe-wearing period.

Ready to try this yourself? Find two to three paragraphs of a longer piece you have written. Or, write from this prompt:

Describe how to navigate to your favorite coffee shop, brew pub, or bakery.

First, write it again in an absurdly formal, elevated tone. Here are a few ideas to inspire you:

- Write it as a pseudo-legal document

- Write it as a graduate textbook entry

- Write as the snobbiest person you can think of

Wander through a thesaurus and search for ornate or unusual words. Go nuts. Don't worry about being ridiculous. That's the point.

Then, write as informally as you can. You might adopt a "folksy" persona or use slang.

Writers who have done this exercise report that they found it fun and useful, if challenging. You may find it sparks creativity and insights into your default writing voice.

The Fancy Version

Write a passage in an absurdly formal or "fancy" voice—whatever that means to you.

_____

_____

_____

_____

_____

_____

_____

_____

_____

_____

_____

The Folksy Version

Revise your paragraphs (or write from the prompt) being as folksy or familiar as possible. Go way beyond what you would ever do.

_____

_____

_____

_____

_____

_____

_____

_____

_____

_____

_____

_____

_____

OBSERVATIONS

• What did this experience teach you?

• If there's a spectrum from folksy to fancy, where does your writing usually fall?

	1	2	3	4	5	
Folksy	○	○	○	○	○	Fancy

What stylistic conventions did you deploy to alter the tone? How did your choices affect elements like:

• sentence length

• punctuation

• word choice

- Was either version longer, or shorter, than the original?

- Did you enjoy pushing the limits?

- Would you want to bring any part of either option into your regular writing routine? Why or why not?

  _____

  _____

- Any other observations from your fancy/folksy stretches?

  » _____

  » _____

  » _____

Expert to Companion

Here's another way to consider your relationship with the reader: are you an expert or a companion in the journey, or both? Are you telling readers what they need to know, or showing them and trusting them to draw their own conclusions?

While this distinction applies most clearly to nonfiction authors, fiction writers face a similar dilemma when deciding exactly how much the narrator knows. Is the narrator omniscient? Do they see only into the main character? Are they themselves a character speaking directly to the reader?

Let's refer to this spectrum of possibilities as *expert to companion.*

This decision links tightly with your choice in Week 9 about presence or absence. It's hard for an absent narrator to be a companion. And although people can (and do) write from the perspective of "I'm the expert and you're not" while remaining present in the work, it's risky. If you don't have a distinctive voice or world-renowned expertise, you may alienate the reader.

To make this decision, you'll need to understand and inhabit your expertise. The genre and medium may affect the results. For example, textbooks generally land on the "expert" side of the spectrum. The writers hope to provide answers. Memoir, personal essay, and first-person narrative nonfiction often treat the reader as a companion rather than a student. Readers travel with the narrator as the work progresses.

Most writing falls in the middle. The writer makes the reader feel present, as a companion, through subtle touches like personal stories, short asides, or humor. The narrator is like a trained and trusted guide on the trail.

Where does your work fall on the spectrum?

Choose your most important writing or current work in progress. On the spectrum from companion to expert, how would you describe your relationship to your reader?

	1	2	3	4	5	
Companion	○	○	○	○	○	Expert

Now write about the same subject in two ways: entirely from a place of expertise, then from a place of companionship. Explore each extreme.

Use excerpts from your own writing or work from the following prompt:

> *Write a few paragraphs convincing a stranger to visit your favorite park or vacation spot.*

Entirely expert version

Entirely companionable version

OBSERVATIONS

- Did being companionable make your voice more or less authoritative, or does it make no difference?

- How did your voice sound while being entirely expert?

- How did working at the extremes affect the decisions you made?

- Based on this experiment, do you want to shift your current, default way of writing in either direction? Why or why not?

■ ■ ■ THIS WEEK:

READING: Use the companion-to-expert gradient to examine texts that you read. As a reader, what do you think of the choices that the writer made?

WRITING: As you write anything from an email to a social media post, first choose a point on the fancy to folksy scale where you want to show up. See if that affects the voice you adopt.

■ ■ ■

WEEK 11

Your Tone, Their Mood

An author once sent me a request to review their book. I did not have the time, so declined and wished them the best in a quick email response. Then I forgot about it. So I was floored when they emailed me back, angered and hurt by my rudeness. Yikes!

Even though we came to peace, the experience still haunts me. How many times have I offended people with my words and not realized it?

Has something like this ever happened to you?

We live very much in our own heads. When I had composed the original, offending email to the author, I felt empathetic and regretful, and assumed my tone would come through. They, however, felt vulnerable in asking for the favor, and perhaps defensive, which may have colored their perception of my response.

Tone is always a negotiation between your intention and the reader's mood.

In a long work like a book, you have time to establish tone. In short posts, articles, and emails, you must be much more explicit. Even then, you can fail.

Psychologists Nicholas Epley and Justin Kruger conducted a test of how well people communicated tone through email—specifically, genuine happiness and sarcasm. Most people thought others would "get" the sarcasm, or lack thereof. Sarcasm and humor are difficult to put down in black and white. The researchers wrote: "People routinely overestimate how well they can communication over e-mail, [...] particularly when the meaning of the message is ambiguous."[10]

Ah, ambiguity! When the mood of a piece is not clear, people contribute their own emotions. And both sides are confident in their interpretations.

---

10 The study "Egocentrism over E-Mail" by J. Kruger, N. Epley, J. Parker and Z.W. NG was published in the *Journal of Personality and Social Psychology* in 2005. Nick Morgan's discusses it in his book *Can You Hear Me?*

You can choose the tone of voice you hope to portray. That's where your control ends. The tone creates a mood for the piece, which the reader senses. Often, though, they bring their own mood to your words.

The reader's contribution may work in your favor. When I (rarely) watch a scary movie, I am so attuned to fear that I readily jump out of my skin at any loud noise in the soundtrack. Likewise, thriller readers show up ready to be frightened.

Readers may bring moods you haven't planned for and don't expect.

How do we reduce the chances for mistaken tone? First, be clear about the tone of voice you plan to convey. Second, double-check how much ambiguity you're leaving in the piece. (We'll practice that in a moment.) We can codify this into two rules:

Rule #1: Target a Specific Tone

The Nielsen Norman Group, a consulting organization focused on user experience, analyzed business writing and suggested four key dimensions of tone of voice in writing:[11]

1. Funny vs. serious

2. Formal vs. casual

3. Respectful vs. irreverent

4. Enthusiastic vs. matter-of-fact

These dimensions apply to business writing, so take them as only a starting point. Fiction may be suspenseful, dark, satirical, poetic, or more. Return to the adjectives you chose in Week 8 for clues about the tone of voice you hope to achieve.

Rule #2: Factor in the Reader's Mood

How will the reader find and approach your work? Might the topic stress them out? There's room for humor in dark subjects, for example, but you'll need to be careful to broadcast your intentions.

PRO TIP: In emails or informal content, make your intended tone clear. For example, include "no sarcasm intended" if you are often snarky, or add stage directions: *[dances with joy]*.

This week's experiments will help you work on both rules.

---

11 An article on the Nielsen Norman Group website describes these dimensions. You can find it at www.nngroup.com/articles/tone-of-voice-dimensions.

Expressing a Clear Tone

In this exercise, you're going to write two short (fictional) emails to colleagues or family members, setting distinctly different moods.

Step 1: Choose the Subject

Pick one of the following subjects.

- Chris left cookies in the breakroom

- A mountain lion was spotted a mile from our house

- Cousin Eddie sent me his latest collection of poems

Got your topic?

Step 2: Write a Joyous Message

Write a quick email about the topic with the subject line *Great News!*

Try to imagine being genuinely happy. No sarcasm, just joy. If you picked a topic that would not make you happy, put yourself in a celebratory mindset. Add as much commentary as seems right.

Subject: Great news! _____

Message: _____

_____

_____

_____

_____

_____

_____

_____

_____

_____

_____

Step 3: Same Topic, Different Tone

Write about the same topic as before, but convey an entirely different emotion. Choose one of the following:

- Sarcastic

- Sorrowful

- Angry

- Awestruck

Use one of the following email subjects based on your chosen mood:

- Sarcastic: Great News

- Sorrowful: Sad News

- Angry or awestruck: Can you believe this?

Subject: _____

Message: _____

_____

_____

_____

_____

_____

_____

_____

_____

_____

_____

_____

_____

OBSERVATIONS

- Did you have fun writing the joyous message?

- Did inhabiting a joyous mood make you more creative?

- How about the other emotions? Writing an angry rant can be fun.

- If you tried sarcasm, how did it differ from the joyous message? Were they close in words, if not intent?

Be a Moody Reader

In the previous exercise, each topic was inherently ambiguous—people might love mountain lions and fear the diet impact of cookies in the break room.

In ambiguous situations, you have to be extra clear. For example, in the last exercise, could you read the joyous email as being sarcastic? People often misinterpret sarcasm.

The study about misinterpreting emails suggested that, to protect against overconfidence, we willfully try to misinterpret tone. We'll try that in this experiment.

Step 1

Choose the happy passage (step 2 of the previous experiment). Now pick an emotion from the following list:

- Fearful

- Angry

- Anxious

- Surprised

- Defensive

- Giddy

Read the "joyous" version of your announcement aloud while inhabiting one of those moods.

Step 2

Choose the second email text (step 3 of the previous exercise) and try reading it aloud using a tone other than the one you intended. If you were awestruck, read it aloud in a sarcastic or sad voice.

OBSERVATIONS

- Was it easy to read the emails in an unintended tone?

- Which combinations of tones were easiest to swap? (Happy/sarcastic? Angry/ awestruck?) _____

- How would you apply this to your own writing voice? Do you ever assume readers will catch your tone?

■ ■ ■ THIS WEEK:

READING: Take a moment during the week to label the tone you perceive when reading pieces: books, blog posts, articles, and emails. How easy or difficult is it to interpret tone? Are your responses ever affected by your mood?

WRITING: As you write, make a quick note of the tone you hope to project. (Refer to your three adjectives from Week 8, if that helps.) Try this on simple writing, like emails, as well as longer works.

■ ■ ■

Moving Closer with Emotion

When I started recording videos for my first online course, a friend watched the video and said, "You look so serious!" Sure enough, I had put on a "serious" face as I spoke to the camera, despite wanting to be warm and supportive.

It didn't really work. My face did not match my intention.

When we're trying hard to do unfamiliar or uncomfortable work, we may show up as anxious, intently focused, nervous, or (in my case) solemn and frowny.

The same thing happens in writing. I've worked with authors with direct, confident speech patterns, who suddenly sound waffly or distant in writing. Any uncertainty about writing itself infuses their voice.

When we sit to write, we may put on a metaphorical "serious writer" hat. This deadens the tone of our words, and often obscures a more authentic voice that would come through and make a stronger connection with the reader. So, lighten up. (Plus, creativity thrives in positive emotional states, so that's another reason to smile!)

Like the major currents beneath the ocean's surface, emotions are invisible forces that guide our actions, behaviors, and communications. They color our writing at every stage, from the birth of an idea to the glimmer of understanding in the reader's mind.

Emotions play a starring role in human communication. Our speaking voices display, and often betray, our feelings. Try giving a reading at a loved one's funeral or listen to a heated conversation in a language you don't understand. Emotions don't need words.

In writing, most emotional cues disappear—the timbre of our voice, facial expressions, and so on. The reader has only the words from which to determine emotion.

There are no emotional vacuums. If your emotional intent isn't clear, readers provide their own.

Spreading Emotions Through Story

In the book *Emotional*, Leonard Moldinow writes, "We now know that we can't make decisions, or even think, without being influenced by our emotions." If you want to reach readers on a deeper level, changing their minds or inspiring them to action, you'll need to make an emotional connection.

The most powerful method for doing this is telling a personal story—one that demonstrates vulnerability and learning.

Story is the vehicle for emotion.

For example, this section began with my short, personal story about my frowny videos. The story was no bigger than it needed to be to serve the message. The point of the story (about our unintended emotional leakage) supports the chapter.

Even if you decide to be fully present in your writing, you choose exactly how intimate you will be with the reader. How much of your inner life should you share? How much will people be comfortable reading? Is a story central to your core message?

Return to your servant authorship statement in Week 7. Will you scare readers off your topic if you share a personal horror story at the start of a book? The story must always serve the reader. And it does that best if it reinforces the message of learning or growth that you hope to share.

You can choose to write about your deepest, most personal experiences. Therapeutic writing is great for mental health. Freewriting and journaling can be remarkably useful. But please, differentiate between your needs, as a writer, and those of the reader.

When writing about sensitive topics, make sure you have a handle on the content before publishing. Examine your motives. Are you trying to cast blame? Are you still feeling defensive or hurt? Those emotions often leak through in the voice, and may not be the emotional connection you hope to make. Don't seek sympathy or redemption. Serve the reader.

Remember, you are still creating a fictional character of yourself, one that includes this (real) personal story.

This week's experiments will challenge you to identify and inhabit emotional states as you write, and then to draft powerful personal stories, which you can choose to share or not. We're going to end our twelve weeks together by getting emotional!

Emotional Drafting

Because our emotions seep through into our speaking and writing voices, the best way to avoid problems and steer your text is by putting yourself in the right emotional state when drafting. You might think of this as inviting the Muse to the process in a specific mood.

This exercise is a companion to last week's experiment on expressing a clear tone. This time, we're going to dig deeper than tone and examine how emotional states affect your writing.

Begin writing in the genre or type of writing you plan to do. If you are a poet, start a poem. A journalist? An article or blog post.

If you are currently working on a project, you may discover approaches and ideas by freewriting on the same topic. (Remember, no one needs to see what you write here.)

Or, use this prompt:

Share a story from your last family holiday.

Before you draft, identify the emotion (one or two, tops) you want the reader to sense from you, the writer. Here are a few options: Love, compassion, pride, anger, contempt, disappointment, sadness, surprise, relief, optimism, excitement, frustration, joy.

Target emotion: _____

Next, spend ten minutes putting yourself into that mood. Some writers use music. Or, tell yourself a story that invokes the mood.

Record what you did to set the mood:

_____

Now draft a few paragraphs on your topic, in that mood. Don't stop and critique, just get the words down without judging.

_____

_____

_____

_____

_____

_____

_____

_____

_____

_____

_____

_____

_____

_____

_____

_____

_____

_____

_____

_____

_____

_____

_____

OBSERVATIONS

- How easy was it to set the right mood?

- What was it like to write in that mood?

Emotions in the Text

Review the paragraphs you wrote in the last exercise. You might let it rest for a day, to get perspective.

First, read it aloud. Does the emotion come through? If you read it in a different emotion, does it still work?

Now look at your instinctive stylistic decisions (sentence, word choice, punctuation) in this emotion and explore how they deviate from your normal writing, if at all.

- Word choices: Did you shift your vocabulary?

- Sentence length: Did your patterns shift?

- Punctuation: Did you shift your use of punctuation?

After waiting a day or two, would you now make any other changes to clarify the emotion in the text?

Gather your observations here for future reference.

Emotional state:_____

How emotion shows up in my writing:

- _____

- _____

- _____

Sticky Stories

If you've ever watched TED talks, you may notice that many of the most popular speakers spend time on a personal story—often a moving description about a vulnerable moment. With so little time in which to spread their message, these speakers commit to a personal story. Emotional stories forge connections with the audience, making them receptive to the rest of the message.

Dr. Nick Morgan is a communication coach who works with public speakers. He encourages speakers to share personal, vulnerable stories when it makes sense for the audience and the purpose. If you hope to inspire people to take action or shift their opinions, forge a stronger bond with a personal story.

Are you uncomfortable sharing your stories? Morgan says, "It may feel risky to tell a personal story and make the emotions as clear as you can. It doesn't feel nearly as risky in the minds of your reader. If you don't feel any risk, chances are you're not sharing much at all."[12]

In this exercise, you're going to tiptoe right up to your "riskiness" border. Don't worry, you won't show this to anyone. It takes practice to get comfortable telling the tough stories of failure or low points. But if the learning or growth will serve others, it's a risk worth taking.

Experiment with that risk here in a story about a difficult time. Even if you don't end up using what you write, the process of putting a narrative around it can be useful. If you write fiction, it may spur a character's story.

Related to your usual writing topics, think of a failure or crisis where you learned an important lesson. Possible prompts:

Describe a moment you wish you could do over.

Share a moment when you felt ashamed or embarrassed (and what you did).

Describe something incredibly foolish you did as a teenager or young adult.

Write as much as you want, a few sentences, a few paragraphs... Open up a journal and let it all out if that's what you need. Identify the key lesson you've taken from the experience, either at the time or now, with the benefit of perspective. It's okay to feel uncomfortable. Keep writing.

---

12 Nick shared this advice with me in a conversation we had. If you're interested in speaking, you should definitely check out his *Just One Question* podcast.

My personal story

_____

_____

_____

_____

_____

_____

_____

_____

_____

_____

_____

_____

_____

_____

_____

_____

_____

OBSERVATIONS

- Whew. Okay, how did that feel? Risky?

- Did you glean any insights into the experience by writing about it?

- Read what you've written aloud. What emotions come through?

- Would you ever share that story in any form? In what circumstances?

- Consider experimenting with personal stories. Over time, you may discover which ones are easier to share than others.

■ ■ ■ THIS WEEK:

READING: Notice whether you can detect distinct emotions in your reading. Much of our online reading is relatively free of explicit emotions. Do pieces that convey an emotion land more deeply with you? If you read a personal story, notice whether it works for you.

WRITING: If you enjoyed the first experiment of setting an emotional tone, see how that helps you work through personal stories. If you're feeling brave, practice writing a few of those personal, emotional stories. Consider creating a file of them, which you may use, now or in the future, in your work.

■ ■ ■

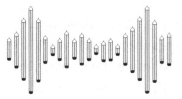

Putting These Techniques to Work

Twelve weeks, dozens of experiments—you now have a bunch of tools that you can add to your writing toolkit.

Here's advice on how to work with these tools in the future.

Tuning Your Own Voice

In my voice survey, many people reported wanting their writing voices to be more compelling, funnier, smoother, or more relaxed. Here's how you might use the techniques in this workbook to make those changes.

Smoother and relaxed: If you want to sound less formal in your writing, think about your relationship with the reader as you write. Play with the folksy-to-fancy spectrum (Week 10). Decide on the tone you want to convey (Week 11) and inhabit a positive mood while drafting (Week 12).

Once the draft is on the page, set the Scribe to work revising. Consider using shorter sentences and words. Look at word choices, and pay attention to the rhythm of the work. Check the Reading Level (Week 6) as a guardrail.

Beautiful/literary/poetic: If you want to write more poetic or literary prose, get the Muse in the mood by tuning your emotion before writing (Week 12). Get a firm sense of the literary voice you want to inhabit (Week 8, You as a Fictional Character). Once you've got a draft, set the Scribe to work on making it sing. Engage the inner reader and listen to the work (Week 1). Vary the rhythm of your sentences (Week 4). Find words that sing (Week 2).

Compelling or riveting: If you want to catch people's attention, start by understanding the audience you serve (Week 7.) Then identify the emotional state and tone you want to convey (Weeks 11 and 12). Once you have a draft, listen to your work (Week 1) so you can learn to grab the attention of the reader's inner narrator. Pay attention to the rhythm of sentences (Week 4) and sounds of words (Week 1). Aim for the unexpected.

Ghostwriting

If you ghostwrite for other people, you'll have happier clients if you can land on a voice that they believe represents them. That work should happen before you write a word. Use these techniques to guide the ghostwriting project.

First, clearly establish who they are serving and why using the Servant Authorship questions in Week 7. Then dive deeper into their relationship with the reader (Week 10). How present do they want to be in the work (Week 9)?

Ask the client for their three adjectives (Week 8). Based on those adjectives, decide about punctuation—do dashes or semicolons make sense for this person? (See Week 3.) While you can make these decisions in revision, it's easier if you know them ahead of time.

Using Week 10's exercises, decide where the subject falls on the folksy-to-fancy and expert-to-companion spectrums.

Ghostwriting Checklist

Client Adjectives:

1._____

2._____

3._____

Punctuation preferences? _____

Pronoun preferences (you/me)? _____

	1	2	3	4	5	
Absence	◯	◯	◯	◯	◯	Presence

	1	2	3	4	5	
Folksy	◯	◯	◯	◯	◯	Fancy

	1	2	3	4	5	
Companion	◯	◯	◯	◯	◯	Expert

Also fill out the servant authorship statement. (See Week 7 or download one from AnneJanzer.com/resources)

Brand Voice

Businesses often have style guides that codify these decisions for people who need to write in a brand voice. If not, make one. The style guide should include:

- The three adjectives: How does the brand want to show up?

- Relationship to reader: Is the brand a trusted guide? An expert?

- Presence and intimacy: Decide about pronoun use.

- Reading level: Set a target reading level based on your core market and try to stay at or below it. The reading level, of course, will affect decisions about sentence length and word length.

Brand Voice Checklist

Brand Adjectives:

1. _____

2. _____

3. _____

Punctuation preferences? _____

Pronoun preferences (you/me)? _____

	1	2	3	4	5	
Absence	○	○	○	○	○	Presence
Folksy	○	○	○	○	○	Fancy
Companion	○	○	○	○	○	Expert

Target reading level: _____

Fictional Characters

If you write fictional characters, you'll want to return to Week 8 and sketch out what's unique about each character's voice. From there, you can identify the sentence structures, word choices, even punctuation that each character would embody.

Fictional Character Checklist

For each character:

Character Adjectives:

1._____

2._____

3._____

Punctuation preferences? _____

Unique tone or character? _____

The Occasional Refresher or Spark of Inspiration

Just as the human speaking voice shifts over time, so does the writing voice. As writers, we are always evolving. The work on our craft never ends.

Every time I do one of the exercises in this book, I learn something, even if I've done it multiple times before. I hope you'll have a similar experience. Perhaps you'll pick this book up again in a few months, open up to an exercise, and give it another shot from a fresh perspective or on a new piece of work.

We're never done tuning our writing voice. Like our physical voice, it shifts with our surroundings and our changing inner landscapes. Writing voice is a work in progress, like our lives. May you enjoy working on yours.

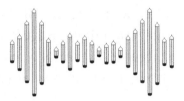

What About AI?

Your writing voice is part of the human connection of writing. So, where does generative artificial intelligence (AI) fit into this equation?[13]

AI-based tools can be invaluable companions in your writing life. Excellent applications include:

- A brainstorming buddy for your Muse

- A research assistant for your Scribe, summarizing articles or studies

- A grammar and spelling checker (AI has been part of these programs for years)

How about voice?

I believe that voice is part of the human connection of writing. We lose trust in the trusting writer/reader relationship if we cede our half of the conversation to a machine. However, AI *can* help us learn about the art and practice of writing voice. Here are a few ideas of ways to incorporate AI into your voice explorations.

Ask AI to evaluate voice in other works. Ask an AI program or chatbot to assess the writing style of authors you admire, providing it a representative passage to work from. You could ask it to identify overall style, as well as specifics like vocabulary, rhetorical devices, and more.

Ask it to assess your work. Provide a passage of writing and describe the purpose of the piece: novel excerpt, personal essay for a specific publication, professional blog post, casual email, and so on. Prompt it to assess the style and tone it perceives as you did above. Compare the results to the three adjectives you identified in Week 8. Does the style perceived match your intentions?

---

13 Artificial intelligence has long been part of writing tools like grammar checkers and auto-complete on your phone. Here, I'm discussing the various "generative" AI tools and chatbots based on large language models.

Have it apply a voice and see what it does: Returning to your three adjectives, ask AI to write a passage in that style. Either give it a prompt for a project you're working on or provide it with your rough draft and ask for a rewrite using a specific voice. After the first pass, you might ask it to take another pass with even more: funnier, more serious, more formal, more authoritative, and so on. It's easier to see what's happening when you look at extreme cases, as we have found in the exercises.

Do you like the result? If so, pay close attention to what's on the page and what you can learn from it:

- The rhythm of the piece: Read it aloud and decide what you think.

- Word choice: Did it rely on specific words to communicate style?

- Sentence length: What type of sentence rhythm did it create?

- Paragraph length: How did it break up the sentences into paragraphs?

Note also that you may not like what it creates as much as your own writing. Then again, it might throw in a phrase that delights you. Learn from that.

Use it to generate your own writing exercises. We often learn through imitation, and AI can help. Use an AI program to generate a summary of a passage from a writer you admire. Then, wait a day or so until you forget the exact wording of the original, look at the summary, and try to recreate the passage in the original author's style. You'll learn something and exercise your writing voice.

You may find many more ways to use AI as a style coach or a supporting tool as you develop and stretch your voice. Or, you can choose to ignore it altogether.

No matter what you do, I encourage you to internalize your voice rather than relying on software to write for you. The second path may be easier and faster, but the first will be more meaningful.

After all, we write to connect with other people. So let them hear your voice.

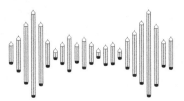

Closing Assessment

Whether you spent a full twelve weeks with this workbook or raced through it at warp speed, you've encountered a lot of ideas for managing your writing voice.

Having done the exercises in this book, how much control do you think you have over your writing voice, on a scale of 1 to 5, with 1 being no control and 5 being complete control.

	1	2	3	4	5	
No control	○	○	○	○	○	Complete control

Compare this to your answer in the Initial Self-Assessment. Do you think you have more control now?

Which exercises will become part of your regular writing routine?

1. _____

2. _____

3. _____

Which will you revisit when you need inspiration?

1. _____

2. _____

3. _____

Which taught you the most about your default writing style?

1. _____

2. _____

3. _____

Which taught you the most about how to tune and adjust your personal style?

1. _____

2. _____

3. _____

Download a complete list of the techniques from AnneJanzer.com/resources. You can print and post it as a reminder of what to do when you want to vary your voice.

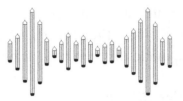

Acknowledgments

Reading the acknowledgements to *any* book gives the lie to the idea of writing as a solitary act.

All books are team efforts, of course. This one, with its interactive exercises, is no exception.

At this point in my writing career, a list of everyone I am indebted to would fill its own book. So, instead of simply listing names, I offer a useful list of kinds of people that writers of all types should look for in their lives, with examples from my own. If you've read this far, maybe you'll find it a helpful nudge to get up from the desk and reach out.

Early testers and readers

These people help give focus to our work, and interact with it at its earliest stages. This book benefitted from both.

I am deeply thankful to my writing friends who volunteered to test my voice-related exercises—and my apologies for swamping your email! Your feedback, comments, and support were priceless, and helped to spark this book in its current form. Special thanks to Marva Bailer, Chris Boutté, Emma Catlin, Karen Catlin, Emilia D'Anzica, M.B. Deans, Gloria Feldt, Meredith Fidrocki, Timothy Gaiser, Marge Johnsson, Dawn Kristy, LaPora Lindsey, Ann Louden, Aidan McCullen, Gerry Paran, Joy Rains, Lori Richardson, Maura Sullivan, Joanne Telser-Frere, Donna Weber, and Emily Wong.

Early readers offer initial support and guidance. My list includes Brad Ferris, Ben Riggs, Chip Scanlan, Evelyn Starr, and Emily Wong again.

Inspiring experts

We always learn from others. In addition to the countless writers who share their experience, a few other experts contributed directly to this work.

I am indebted to Dr. Nick Morgan for his insights into communication, both spoken and written, and Ann Handley for sharing her unique approach to style. Sam Horn has inspired my fun with alliteration and rhyming. Erin Lebacqz's valuable insight as a teacher of writing made this book much better.

Guides to new technologies (like AI)

Surround yourself with people who stay tuned to the changing world.

Many friends and experts have helped me shape my understanding of AI in writing, including Pamela Wilson, Dan Janal, and Alastair McDermott. Mark Janzer taught me how to interact with ChatGPT and also offered the idea for creating summaries of famous works to test writing in different styles.

A great publishing team

My publishing team has pulled through once again to create something special: Laurie Gibson and Mark Rhynsburger have turned their critical eyes to the words. Any mistakes that snuck through into the text result from my stubborn inability to stop tinkering with the prose. Carla Green designed a wonderful cover and a beautiful interior rich with interactive elements and pleasing pages. It's hard to make a book feel interactive, and she has risen to the challenge.

Communities of authors and writers

We all benefit from the support of others, whether they are literally by our side or have our back online.

I draw constant support and inspiration from my author communities, including the marvelous Authoresses and Melissa Wilson's Author Support Circle. My coaching clients inevitably teach me a great deal about their subjects and writing itself. It's a privilege to connect with so many wise and wonderful writers.

The writers in my Writing Practices list constantly inspire and motivate me. You might be surprised by the impact a few kind words in email can have on a toiling writer.

A supportive home team

With people who believe in you, you can focus on serving those who need what you have to say.

Every day, I am grateful for the support and patience of my family and especially my husband, Steve.

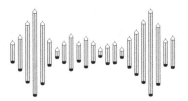

Further Reading

So many wonderful writers, teachers, and thinkers have contributed their opinions on voice that it's nearly impossible to untangle the sources.

Here are a few books if you're interested in diving deeper into the various aspects of writing voice. All have influenced me.

- The evolution of language: *The Language Game* by Morten H. Christiansen and Nick Chater

- Classic writing style: *Clear and Simple as the Truth* by Francis-Noël Thomas and Mark Turner

- Freewriting: *Exploratory Writing* by Alison Jones

- Literary voice: *The Sound on the Page* by Ben Yagoda

- Poetic voice: *The Art of Voice* by Tony Hoagland

- Public writing: *Tell It Like It Is* by Roy Peter Clark

- Punctuation: *Confessions of a Comma Queen* by Mary Norris

- Reading as a cognitive act: *Reader, Come Home* by Maryanne Wolf

- Virtual communication: *Can You Hear Me* by Nick Morgan

- Writing for business: *Everybody Writes* by Ann Handley and *High Value Writing* by Erin Lebacqz

About the Author

Anne Janzer is a nonfiction book coach and the author of multiple award-winning books on writing, including *The Writer's Process* and *Writing to Be Understood*. Human behavior and cognitive science fascinate her, and she is always searching for clues to improving our communication.

As a book coach, she guides authors using the concept of servant authorship, or writing to serve a specific group of people with a meaningful message. And she loves talking about the geeky aspects of writing and communicating.

If you enjoy this combination of inner and outer work, of science and literary experiments, please join her Writing Practices List at AnneJanzer.com. You'll get every-other-week writing advice, plus drawings for writing-related books and more.

■ ■ ■

You can exercise your writing skills right away on a quick book review! Reviews help others find the work. I would be deeply grateful if you leave an honest review wherever you buy books.

Made in United States
North Haven, CT
16 June 2024

53703185R00083